NEW MEXICO TRIVIA

NEW MEXICO TRIVIA

COMPILED BY ROBERT ELLIS, MARY CLARK,
AND JIM CLARK

Rutledge Hill Press
Nashville, Tennessee

Published in Nashville, Tennessee, by Rutledge Hill Press,
211 Seventh Avenue North, Nashville, Tennessee 37219.
Distributed in Canada by H. B. Fenn & Company, Ltd.,
1090 Lorimar Drive, Mississauga, Ontario L5S 1R7.

Typography by D&T/Bailey Typesetting, Inc., Nashville, Tennessee.
Cover design by Linda Nelson

Library of Congress Cataloging-in-Publication Data

Ellis, Robert, 1967–
    New Mexico trivia / compiled by Robert Ellis, Mary Clark, and
Jim Clark.
    p.   cm.
    ISBN 1-55853-380-X (pbk.)
    1. New Mexico—Miscellanea.   I. Clark, Mary, 1963–   .
II. Clark, Jim, 1960–   .   III. Title.
F796.E44 1996   96-2092
978.9—dc20   CIP

Printed in the United States of America.
1 2 3 4 5 6 7 8 — 99 98 97 96

PREFACE

We have compiled this book with the hope that it will give you an engaging glimpse into the fascinating world of our beloved state. As you roam through this collection, you'll discover a New Mexico that is chock-full of facts to entertain you, test your knowledge, and spur New Mexico residents and visitors alike to learn more about one of the most spectacular places on earth.

Because New Mexico is blessed with such an interesting diversity of cultures and happenings, it's a challenge for any book to explore all that there is to know about this magnificent land and its people. So follow your curiosity and have fun pursuing the many rewarding horizons of New Mexico!

Robert Ellis, Mary Clark, & Jim Clark

To Mary, Jim, and Jane Ellis,
and
the enchanting people of New Mexico

TABLE OF CONTENTS

GEOGRAPHY

C H A P T E R   O N E

Q. What are New Mexico's three most populated cities?

A. Albuquerque, Santa Fe, and Las Cruces.

———◆———

Q. What is the state's highest mountain?

A. Wheeler Peak, at 13,161 feet.

———◆———

Q. What is New Mexico's only natural boundary with another state?

A. A fifteen-mile section of the Rio Grande along the southern border with Texas.

———◆———

Q. What university was established in 1893 in Silver City?

A. Western New Mexico University.

———◆———

Q. What four towns in the state have the fewest letters in their names?

A. Abo, Jal, Lea, and Roy.

Q. What is the state's most populated pueblo?

A. Zuni.

◆

Q. Who is Santa Fe's patron saint?

A. Saint Francis of Assisi.

◆

Q. What is the largest Indian tribe in both New Mexico and the United States?

A. Navajo, with about 78,000 members in New Mexico and 200,000 members nationwide.

◆

Q. Where is the original Spanish city of "Alburquerque" located?

A. In the province Badajoz near the Portuguese border in western Spain.

◆

Q. "To-Tah," the Indian name for Farmington, means what?

A. Place Among Waters.

◆

Q. In what city do Interstates 40 and 25 intersect?

A. Albuquerque.

◆

Q. What mountains serve as a backdrop for Las Cruces?

A. Organ Mountains.

Q. What is Inscription Rock?

A. A great monolith of sandstone, southwest of Grants, also known as El Morro, on which everyone from Indians and conquistadors to missionaries and outlaws has carved his or her name.

———◆———

Q. What are the names of the two large pueblos in Bandelier National Park?

A. Tyuonyi and Tsonkawi.

———◆———

Q. What is the Enchanted Circle?

A. A loop road north of Taos.

———◆———

Q. What city hosts the New Mexico State Fair every September?

A. Albuquerque.

———◆———

Q. What is the elevation of Bernalillo?

A. 5,050 feet.

———◆———

Q. What city took its name from a popular radio game show of the 1950s?

A. Truth or Consequences.

———◆———

Q. What city was home of Walker Air Base?

A. Roswell.

Q. In what year was the earliest map of "Villa de Alburquerque" drawn by Fr. Francisco Kino?

A. 1724.

◆

Q. What city is home to New Mexico State University?

A. Las Cruces.

◆

Q. Where was the 1950s western TV show *Law of the Plainsman* set?

A. Santa Fe.

◆

Q. The Pecos River is a tributary of what river?

A. Rio Grande.

◆

Q. Where did the town of Folsom get its name?

A. In honor of Frances Folsom, who married President Grover Cleveland.

◆

Q. What is unusual about the location of Abo Elementary School in Artesia?

A. It is underground.

◆

Q. What city, founded in 1927, is known as the Oil Capital of New Mexico?

A. Hobbs.

Q. What national forest is home to New Mexico's Wheeler Peak?

A. Carson National Forest.

Q. What body of water in the state did the Goodnight-Loving Trail follow?

A. Pecos River.

Q. Where is the Federal Law Enforcement Training Center (FLETC) located?

A. Artesia, on the grounds of the former Artesian Christian College.

Q. What is the total acreage of the Mescalero Apache Indian Reservation?

A. 472,320.

Q. What is the southernmost peak in the United States to reach the Arctic Alpine Life Zone in altitude?

A. Sierra Blanca, with an elevation of 12,003 feet.

Q. How long is the Jemez Mountain chain?

A. Forty miles.

Q. Paseo del Norte roadway on the west side of Albuquerque runs into what national monument?

A. Petroglyph National Monument.

Q. What is the name of the rounded and layered mound that rises three hundred feet above the surrounding valley near Clayton?

A. Wedding Cake.

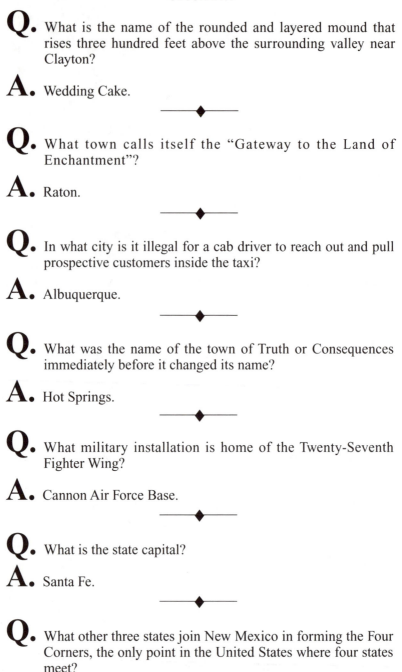

Q. What town calls itself the "Gateway to the Land of Enchantment"?

A. Raton.

Q. In what city is it illegal for a cab driver to reach out and pull prospective customers inside the taxi?

A. Albuquerque.

Q. What was the name of the town of Truth or Consequences immediately before it changed its name?

A. Hot Springs.

Q. What military installation is home of the Twenty-Seventh Fighter Wing?

A. Cannon Air Force Base.

Q. What is the state capital?

A. Santa Fe.

Q. What other three states join New Mexico in forming the Four Corners, the only point in the United States where four states meet?

A. Arizona, Colorado, and Utah.

Q. What international crime prevention program was started in Albuquerque in 1976 by police detective Greg MacAleese?

A. Crime Stoppers.

Q. What is the elevation of Taos?

A. 7,000 feet.

Q. Where is the main campus of Eastern New Mexico State University?

A. Portales.

Q. What is the longest river in the state?

A. Rio Grande.

Q. At an elevation of 13,110 feet, Truchas Peak is part of what mountain group?

A. Sangre de Cristo Mountains.

Q. What New Mexico city was named for three brothers?

A. Grants.

Q. What pueblo is also known as Sky City?

A. Acoma.

Q. What is the second highest bridge of the national highway system?

A. Rio Grande Gorge Bridge.

———◆———

Q. How did Hermit's Peak, just over a mile south of Las Vegas, New Mexico, get its name?

A. From a religious hermit who is said to have lived at the base of the peak for several years during the nineteenth century.

———◆———

Q. Sandoval County is home to which two of the state's five state monuments?

A. Coronado State Monument and Jemez State Monument.

———◆———

Q. What are the only two counties in the state that are bordered on two sides by Texas?

A. Lea and Doña Ana.

———◆———

Q. Where in New Mexico was the first Spanish colony in what is now the United States?

A. San Gabriel.

———◆———

Q. If you were living in "fat cottonwood" where would you be?

A. Alamogordo.

———◆———

Q. What is the elevation of Sandia Crest?

A. 10,678 feet.

Q. From whom did the San Juan County's Salmon Ruin get its name?

A. George Salmon, a homesteader of the late nineteenth century.

◆

Q. New Mexico Boys School is located in what town?

A. Springer.

◆

Q. What do Kelly, Shakespeare, Steins, Chloride, and Colfax have in common?

A. They are all ghost towns.

◆

Q. What is Whitewater Baldy?

A. An 11,000-foot peak in the Gila National Forest.

◆

Q. What New Mexico county is the largest in land size?

A. Catron.

◆

Q. Besides being a hideout for Butch Cassidy and the Wild Bunch, Whitewater Canyon served as a sanctuary for what Indian chief?

A. Geronimo.

◆

Q. What was the smallest city honored with the designation as a 1994 All-America City?

A. Taos.

Q. What is the lowest point in New Mexico?

A. Red Bluff Reservoir, at an elevation of 2,817 feet.

Q. How many counties are in the state?

A. Thirty-three.

Q. What is the second largest body of impounded water in the world?

A. Elephant Butte Lake, near Truth or Consequences.

Q. What is the county seat of Torrance County?

A. Estancia.

Q. Where is the only Merchant Marine cemetery in the United States located?

A. Fort Stanton.

Q. Where is the Old Mill Museum?

A. Cimarron.

Q. What is the largest city located in the area called Agua Negra Chiquita (Little Black Water) by Spanish explorer Antonio de Espejo?

A. Santa Rosa.

Q. For what Indian chief is a mineral spring in Truth or Consequences named because he often stopped there to relax?

A. Geronimo.

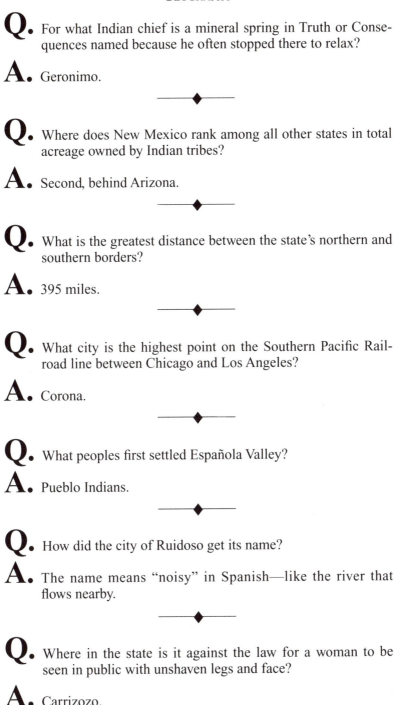

Q. Where does New Mexico rank among all other states in total acreage owned by Indian tribes?

A. Second, behind Arizona.

Q. What is the greatest distance between the state's northern and southern borders?

A. 395 miles.

Q. What city is the highest point on the Southern Pacific Railroad line between Chicago and Los Angeles?

A. Corona.

Q. What peoples first settled Española Valley?

A. Pueblo Indians.

Q. How did the city of Ruidoso get its name?

A. The name means "noisy" in Spanish—like the river that flows nearby.

Q. Where in the state is it against the law for a woman to be seen in public with unshaven legs and face?

A. Carrizozo.

Q. Why is Jornado del Muerto (Journey of Death) an appropriate name for the route heading north from Hatch?

A. It is a demanding desert route on which unprepared travelers of yesteryear faced the prospect of dying from thirst.

Q. The Village of Rodey used to be known by what other name?

A. Colorado.

Q. What famous New Mexico sheriff's ranch was located on the eastern side of the San Andres Mountains?

A. Pat Garrett.

Q. In 1861–62, during the Confederate Occupation, Mesilla was the capital of what territory?

A. Arizona.

Q. What county is home of the Mescalero Apache Indian Reservation?

A. Otero.

Q. What county produces most of the state's zinc?

A. Grant.

Q. Where is New Mexico Highlands University?

A. Las Vegas.

Q. What happened to New Mexico land with the Treaty of Guadalupe-Hidalgo?

A. It was ceded to the United States by Mexico.

———◆———

Q. McMillan Dam is on what river?

A. Pecos.

———◆———

Q. Don Antonio de Espejo blazed what important route in 1582?

A. El Camino Real.

———◆———

Q. For whom is the city of Clovis named?

A. The first Christian king of the Frankish Empire.

———◆———

Q. The Guadalupe Mountains are part of what larger mountain range?

A. Sacramento Mountains.

———◆———

Q. How many New Mexico counties ranked among the fifty most racially diverse counties in the 1990 U.S. Census?

A. Five.

———◆———

Q. Mountain Branch and Cimarron Cut-Off were part of what larger route?

A. Santa Fe Trail.

Q. Most transcontinental freight trains go through what city?

A. Belen, site of the state's largest freight classification yard.

Q. What is Chaco Canyon's nickname?

A. Stonehenge of the Southwest.

Q. What city got its name from a cowboy campsite where spring water came up from a string of caves that look like front porches?

A. Portales.

Q. The Chili Line, built by the Denver and Rio Grande Western Railroad, connected what two cities?

A. Española, New Mexico, and Antonito, Colorado.

Q. Tijeras (scissors) Canyon is between what two mountains named for fruit?

A. Sandia (watermelon) and Manzano (apple) mountains.

Q. What New Mexico county was the nation's largest at the turn of the twentieth century?

A. Lincoln.

Q. What route is known as "the low road to Taos"?

A. Highway 68.

Q. What is the capital of the Jicarilla Apache Reservation?

A. Dulce.

Q. Where is Pancho Villa State Park?

A. Columbus.

Q. What town's name is an acronym?

A. Jal (for cattle rancher John A. Lynch).

Q. What ancient New Mexico city was the first of the Seven Cities of Gold?

A. Hawikuh.

Q. What is the shortest name of a county in the state?

A. Lea.

Q. What city has been home of the All-Indian Pueblo Cultural Center since 1976?

A. Albuquerque.

Q. Where does New Mexico rank in size among other U.S. states?

A. Fifth.

Q. Where does New Mexico rank in water area size among the fifty states?

A. Fiftieth.

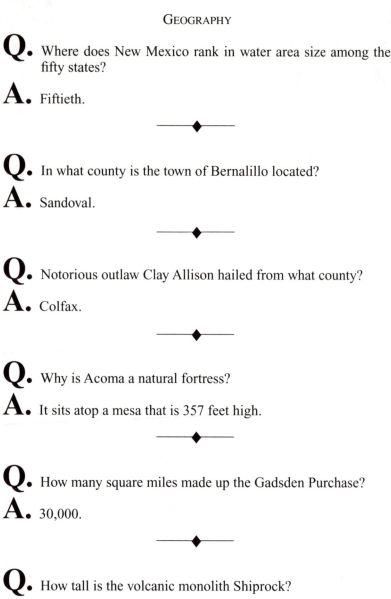

Q. In what county is the town of Bernalillo located?

A. Sandoval.

Q. Notorious outlaw Clay Allison hailed from what county?

A. Colfax.

Q. Why is Acoma a natural fortress?

A. It sits atop a mesa that is 357 feet high.

Q. How many square miles made up the Gadsden Purchase?

A. 30,000.

Q. How tall is the volcanic monolith Shiprock?

A. 1,700 feet.

Q. In what time zone do New Mexicans live?

A. Mountain.

Q. What was the previous name for the town of Folsom?

A. Ragtown.

Q. What is the biggest employer of civilians in Portales?

A. Eastern New Mexico State University.

Q. What city, at an elevation of 4,000 feet and founded in 1741, is a terminal point for the Santa Fe Railway and takes its name from the Spanish word for Bethlehem?

A. Belen.

Q. If you were to depart from an unknown point in New Mexico and were to head east, west, south, or north, what are the only two directions you could go and be sure that there was the possibility of your entering only one other state?

A. West to Arizona or north to Colorado.

Q. What is the oldest road in the state?

A. El Camino Real (U.S. 85).

Q. How long is New Mexico's Enchanted Circle loop?

A. Eighty-five miles.

Q. From what does the town of Acme take its name?

A. Acme Cement Company.

Q. What is unique about New Mexico's name among the fifty states?

A. It is the only state name to be taken in part from the name of another country.

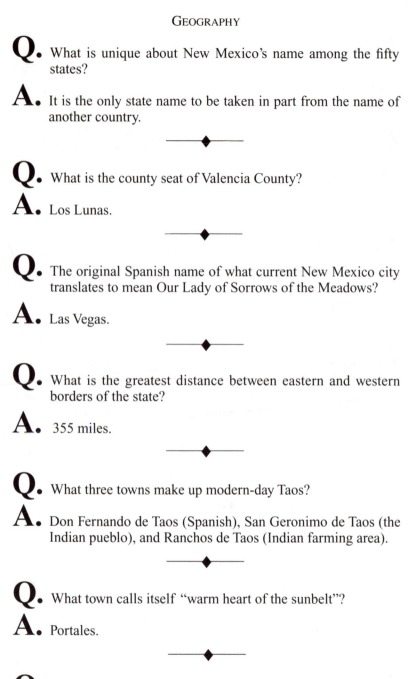

Q. What is the county seat of Valencia County?

A. Los Lunas.

Q. The original Spanish name of what current New Mexico city translates to mean Our Lady of Sorrows of the Meadows?

A. Las Vegas.

Q. What is the greatest distance between eastern and western borders of the state?

A. 355 miles.

Q. What three towns make up modern-day Taos?

A. Don Fernando de Taos (Spanish), San Geronimo de Taos (the Indian pueblo), and Ranchos de Taos (Indian farming area).

Q. What town calls itself "warm heart of the sunbelt"?

A. Portales.

Q. By what name was Clovis known until 1907?

A. Riley's Switch.

Q. What town is known as the Chile Capital of the World?

A. Hatch.

Q. Greer Garson's Fogelson Ranch is now part of what national park?

A. Pecos National Historical Park.

Q. In what New Mexico city did Armand Hammer establish his United World College?

A. Las Vegas.

Q. Uncle Dick Wootton set up a toll booth after he dynamited what location to make travel easier for wagon traffic?

A. Raton Pass.

Q. In what county are the Three Rivers Petroglyphs located?

A. Otero.

Q. Truth or Consequences is the third name of a town in the southern part of the state, but what was the location's original name?

A. Province of San Felipe.

Q. Clayton is at the foot of what mountain range?

A. Rabbit Ear Mountains.

Q. How many states have elevations higher than New Mexico's highest point?

A. Seven (Alaska, California, Colorado, Washington, Wyoming, Hawaii, and Utah).

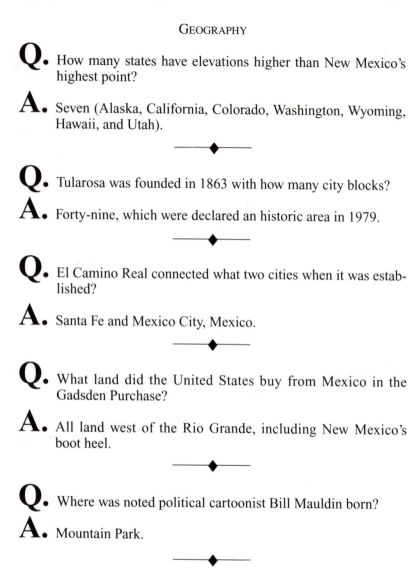

Q. Tularosa was founded in 1863 with how many city blocks?

A. Forty-nine, which were declared an historic area in 1979.

Q. El Camino Real connected what two cities when it was established?

A. Santa Fe and Mexico City, Mexico.

Q. What land did the United States buy from Mexico in the Gadsden Purchase?

A. All land west of the Rio Grande, including New Mexico's boot heel.

Q. Where was noted political cartoonist Bill Mauldin born?

A. Mountain Park.

Q. The village of Cloudcroft is located in what mountains?

A. Sacramento Mountains.

Q. America's longest and highest narrow gauge steam railroad connects what two cities?

A. Chama, New Mexico, and Antonito, Colorado.

Q. What do Governor Don Juan de Oñate, Peachy Breckinridge, and Gen. Diego de Vargas have in common?

A. Each made his mark on Inscription Rock.

Q. What was the largest town in the state at the end of the nineteenth century?

A. Las Vegas.

Q. Approximately what percentage of the state's landscape is lakes, rivers, and streams?

A. About two percent (roughly 225 square miles).

Q. What is the only town in the United States ever invaded by a foreign army?

A. Columbus (by Mexico's Pancho Villa).

Q. How high above the river is the Rio Grande Gorge Bridge?

A. 650 feet.

Q. How large is New Mexico in square miles?

A. 121,666.

Q. How many non-New Mexico governments share an eastern border with the state?

A. Three (Oklahoma, Texas, and Mexico).

Q. What is the geographic center of the state?

A. Twelve miles south-southwest of Willard, in Torrance County.

Q. From whom did the Gadsden Purchase, which involved New Mexico land, get its name?

A. James Gadsden, U.S. negotiator for the deal.

Q. What interstate highways completely cross the state?

A. I-25 from north to south and I-40 from east to west.

Q. What is the tallest building in the state?

A. The twenty-two story Albuquerque Plaza, which rises 302½ feet above ground.

Q. Where did the town of Magdalena get its name?

A. The mountain overlooking the town has a rock formation thought to bear Mary Magdalene's likeness.

Q. Where did the Sandia Mountains get their name?

A. From the Spanish description of the watermelon pink color that they appear to be at sunset.

Q. What town, a setting for numerous motion pictures, reached its peak in the 1880s with twenty-one saloons and four hotels?

A. Cerrillos.

Q. What is the elevation of Tucumcari Mountain?

A. 4,967 feet.

———◆———

Q. How long is Conchas Dam, one of the longest in the world?

A. 3½ miles.

———◆———

Q. How did the Goodnight Trail get its name?

A. From Charles Goodnight, who blazed the trail in 1866.

———◆———

Q. What village along the Turquoise Trail is aptly named after the first gold rush west of the Mississippi?

A. Golden.

———◆———

Q. How big is the Navajo Indian Reservation in the Four Corners area?

A. 25,000 square miles.

———◆———

Q. What town in the southeastern part of the state has a man-made lake that spells out its name?

A. Jal.

———◆———

Q. Where did Artesia get its name?

A. From area artesian wells.

Q. What three rivers converge near Española?

A. Rio Grande, Rio Chama, and Santa Cruz.

———◆———

Q. Where in the state can you walk into a volcano?

A. Capulin Volcano, one of the few places in the world where you can do so.

———◆———

Q. What livestock drive on the San Augustin Plains was used from 1880–1969 and was one hundred miles long and ten miles wide?

A. Magdalena Driveway.

———◆———

Q. What percentage of the state is timbered?

A. Approximately twenty-five.

———◆———

Q. How did the village of Rodey get its name?

A. From Bernard S. Rodey, who battled in Congress for state-hood.

———◆———

Q. How many acres make up the Bandelier National Monument?

A. 32,734.

———◆———

Q. What is Santa Rosa's Blue Hole?

A. An eighty-one-foot deep natural artesian spring that delivers up to three thousand gallons of water per minute.

Q. Who established the settlement of San Gabriel in 1598?

A. Don Juan de Oñate.

———◆———

Q. What is the southernmost national forest in the state?

A. Coronado National Forest.

———◆———

Q. How long is the Rio Grande Valley?

A. 2,200 miles.

———◆———

Q. What site of a great lava flow in the state is one of the most recently formed in the continental United States?

A. Malpais Lava Beds.

———◆———

Q. The community of Mills is in the heart of what nationally protected area?

A. Kiowa National Grasslands.

———◆———

Q. Interstate 10 and Interstate 25 intersect in what city?

A. Las Cruces.

———◆———

Q. Does rainwater in Grants drain generally to the east or to the west of town?

A. East, following the inclination of the Continental Divide.

Q. The town of Lakewood is next to what body of water?

A. Brantley Reservoir.

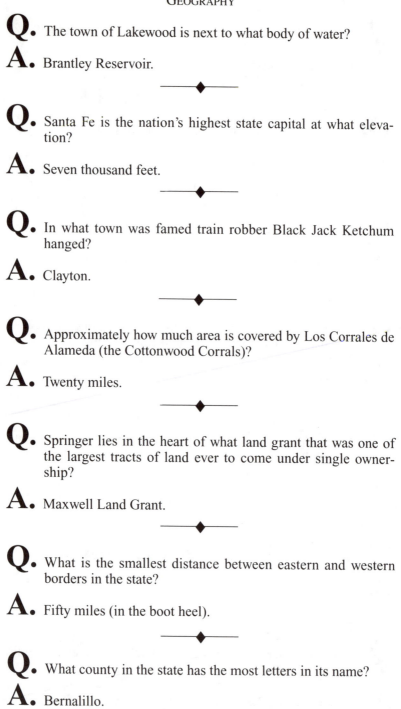

Q. Santa Fe is the nation's highest state capital at what elevation?

A. Seven thousand feet.

Q. In what town was famed train robber Black Jack Ketchum hanged?

A. Clayton.

Q. Approximately how much area is covered by Los Corrales de Alameda (the Cottonwood Corrals)?

A. Twenty miles.

Q. Springer lies in the heart of what land grant that was one of the largest tracts of land ever to come under single ownership?

A. Maxwell Land Grant.

Q. What is the smallest distance between eastern and western borders in the state?

A. Fifty miles (in the boot heel).

Q. What county in the state has the most letters in its name?

A. Bernalillo.

Q. What popular and unusual rock formations are about thirty miles south of Farmington?

A. Bisti Badlands.

Q. Where does New Mexico rank among the fifty states in total population?

A. Thirty-sixth.

Q. In what Rocky Mountain range is Wheeler Peak?

A. Sangre de Cristo.

Q. What is the dominant direction of the natural flow of the Rio Grande?

A. South.

Q. What Mexican states border New Mexico?

A. Sonora and Chihuahua.

Q. San Juan, Little Colorado, and Gila are tributaries of what river?

A. Colorado.

Q. What broad geographic term describes the terrain of the eastern two-fifths of the state?

A. Great Plains.

Q. For whom was Fort Stanton named?

A. Capt. Henry W. Stanton of the U.S. Army.

Q. Where was longtime U.S. Senator Dennis Chavez born?

A. Los Chavez.

Q. Navajo Dam is on what river?

A. San Juan.

Q. Santa Rita is best known for the mining of what ore?

A. Copper.

Q. Where is St. John's College?

A. Santa Fe.

Q. New Mexico's land size was reduced in 1863 by the formation of what?

A. Territory of Arizona.

Q. The Zuni Indian Reservation is primarily in what county?

A. McKinley.

Q. What desert does New Mexico share with Texas, Arizona, and Mexico?

A. Chihuahuan Desert, North America's largest desert.

Q. What mission between Albuquerque and Santa Fe was built fifteen years before the Pilgrims landed at Plymouth?

A. Santa Domingo.

Q. What city's logo is three crosses?

A. Las Cruces.

Q. The Sangre de Cristo Mountains are the southern end of what chain?

A. The Rockies.

Q. What is considered the "only surviving settlement of the Seven Cities of Cibola"?

A. Zuni.

Q. How big is the impounded body of water, El Vado Lake?

A. 3,200 acres.

Q. What is the population of New Mexico?

A. 1,616,000 and growing, according to a 1993 government estimate.

Q. Is Albuquerque 1,220 miles, 2,220 miles, or 3,220 miles from Boston?

A. 2,220 miles.

———◆———

Q. The Rio Grande empties into what body of water?

A. Gulf of Mexico.

———◆———

Q. What New Mexico town calls itself "City Different"?

A. Santa Fe.

———◆———

Q. What town was home of outlaw-favorite Blancett's Saloon?

A. Bloomfield.

———◆———

Q. How many members of the U.S. House of Representatives does New Mexico have?

A. Three.

ENTERTAINMENT

C H A P T E R   T W O

Q. Nacio Herb Brown of Deming is likely best known for composing what hit song?

A. "Singin' in the Rain."

———◆———

Q. What 1993 film starring Kevin Costner and Gene Hackman was shot at locations throughout the state?

A. *Wyatt Earp.*

———◆———

Q. What popular comic strip was drawn by Tesuque native Bill Watterson until his retirement in 1995?

A. "Calvin & Hobbes."

———◆———

Q. Jodie Foster hides out from and then with Dennis Hopper in New Mexico in what 1989 movie directed by Hopper?

A. *Backtrack.*

———◆———

Q. Where was the video for country singer George Ducas's 1995 hit "Kisses Don't Lie" filmed?

A. White Sands National Monument.

Q. What popular performance takes place in Madrid from Memorial Day through Labor Day?

A. Madrid Melodrama.

———◆———

Q. What 1950 western starring Errol Flynn and Patrice Wymore was filmed in Gallup?

A. *Rocky Mountain.*

———◆———

Q. What was the number one song for 1963 that was recorded in New Mexico at Norman Petty Studios?

A. "Sugarshack" by the Fireballs.

———◆———

Q. What 1971 TV movie starring William Conrad and Vera Miles was about murder and corruption in New Mexico?

A. *Cannon.*

———◆———

Q. Where in New Mexico was the Civil War western *Two Flags West*, starring Dale Robertson and Joseph Cotten, filmed?

A. San Ildefonso.

———◆———

Q. What 1988 western and its 1990 sequel were filmed in the state?

A. *Young Guns* and *Young Guns II.*

———◆———

Q. What New Mexico resident won the 1942 Best Actress Oscar for *Mrs. Miniver*, which also won for Best Picture?

A. Greer Garson.

Q. Why do people join Taiban's Billy the Kid Outlaw Gang?

A. To "preserve, protect, and promote Billy the Kid/Pat Garrett history."

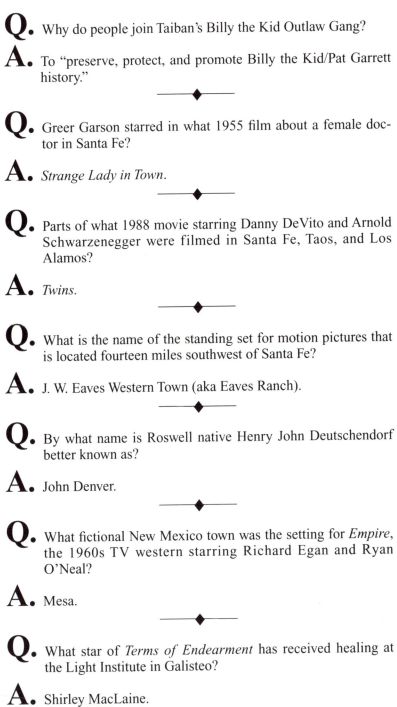

Q. Greer Garson starred in what 1955 film about a female doctor in Santa Fe?

A. *Strange Lady in Town.*

Q. Parts of what 1988 movie starring Danny DeVito and Arnold Schwarzenegger were filmed in Santa Fe, Taos, and Los Alamos?

A. *Twins.*

Q. What is the name of the standing set for motion pictures that is located fourteen miles southwest of Santa Fe?

A. J. W. Eaves Western Town (aka Eaves Ranch).

Q. By what name is Roswell native Henry John Deutschendorf better known as?

A. John Denver.

Q. What fictional New Mexico town was the setting for *Empire*, the 1960s TV western starring Richard Egan and Ryan O'Neal?

A. Mesa.

Q. What star of *Terms of Endearment* has received healing at the Light Institute in Galisteo?

A. Shirley MacLaine.

Q. What 1948 western film starring Randolph Scott and Barbara Britton has a New Mexico city as its title?

A. *Albuquerque.*

Q. In what year did the Santa Fe Opera present its first performance?

A. 1957.

Q. Charles Bronson, Jack Palance, and Jill Ireland starred in what 1972 western about an Apache being chased by a posse in New Mexico?

A. *Chato's Land.*

Q. Who wrote the screenplay for the 1993 film *Blood In, Blood Out*?

A. Santa Fe native Jimmy Santiago Baca.

Q. What was the first production ever presented by the Albuquerque Civic Light Opera Association?

A. *Once Upon a Mattress.*

Q. What 1969 movie starring Robert Mitchum and George Kennedy was filmed near Chama?

A. *The Good Guys and the Bad Guys.*

Q. What Taos singer/songwriter has "Wildfire" among his hits?

A. Michael Martin Murphey.

Q. Where was the 1971 TV movie *The City* filmed?

A. Albuquerque.

Q. In what year was the New Mexico State Film Commission established?

A. In 1968, as the first state film commission in the nation.

Q. Why did the Santa Fe *New Mexican* apologize to the Santa Domingo Indian community in 1984?

A. For publishing two photographs of sacred dances, which is against the community's posted policy.

Q. What 1941 film starring Gene Tierney and New Mexico native Bruce Cabot was shot at Gallup and Acoma Pueblo?

A. *Sundown.*

Q. What is actor/singer Ronny Cox's hometown?

A. Cloudcroft.

Q. What 1972 film starring John Wayne, Slim Pickens, and Bruce Dern was filmed at Chama and Eaves Ranch?

A. *The Cowboys.*

Q. Where in the state did Burl Ives live for many years?

A. Galisteo.

Q. What 1970 blockbuster film was shot in Santa Clara Pueblo, Eaves Ranch, and Bandelier?

A. *Billy Jack.*

———◆———

Q. Who married Georgia Gabor in Santa Fe in 1942 and honeymooned at the Albuquerque Hilton?

A. Conrad Hilton (Georgia became better known as Zsa Zsa).

———◆———

Q. Where in the state were parts of the movie *My Name Is Nobody*, starring Henry Fonda, filmed?

A. Mogollon.

———◆———

Q. What venue hosts the melodramas in Madrid?

A. The Engine House Theater, where a locomotive is the backdrop.

———◆———

Q. What radio show had its first live, coast-to-coast broadcast from New Mexico on April 1, 1950?

A. "Truth or Consequences."

———◆———

Q. *Four Faces West* and *Bad Man* both were filmed where?

A. Gallup.

———◆———

Q. What artist had the first hit record produced at Norman Petty Studios?

A. Buddy Knox with "Party Doll."

Q. What 1960 film starring Richard Basehart and Stuart Erwin is about a Native American boy in New Mexico who cares for his horse?

A. *For the Love of Mike.*

Q. What New Mexico native won the Emmy for outstanding single performance by an actress in a leading role in 1963?

A. Kim Stanley for her work on *Ben Casey.*

Q. Where in the state was the 1914 Tom Mix film *The Rancher's Daughter* filmed?

A. Las Vegas.

Q. "Flibbertigibbet," "Up at State Prison," "A Capella," and "There's My Darling Person" are New Mexico chapters of what national organization?

A. *The Andy Griffith Show* Rerun Watchers Club.

Q. What film starring Roswell's Demi Moore premiered simultaneously in more countries than any previous film?

A. *A Few Good Men,* which premiered in fifty countries in 1992.

Q. Who recorded most of his biggest hits for Norman Petty in Clovis from 1957–59?

A. Buddy Holly.

Q. What 1913 western starring Romaine Fielding was filmed in Las Vegas?

A. *The Rattlesnake.*

Q. Where does National Old Time Fiddlers Association President Wes Nivens live?

A. Truth or Consequences.

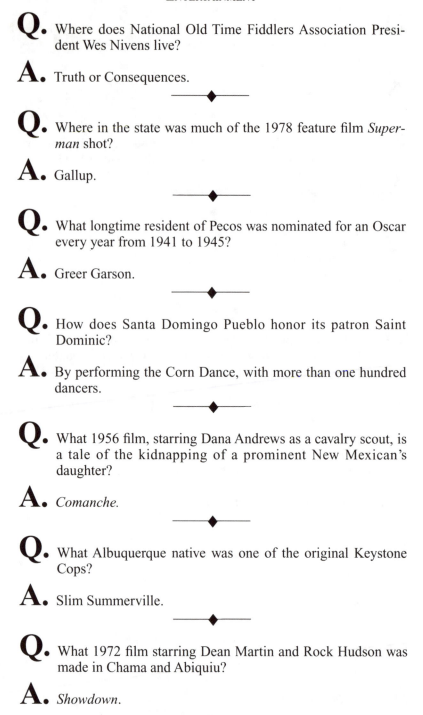

Q. Where in the state was much of the 1978 feature film *Superman* shot?

A. Gallup.

Q. What longtime resident of Pecos was nominated for an Oscar every year from 1941 to 1945?

A. Greer Garson.

Q. How does Santa Domingo Pueblo honor its patron Saint Dominic?

A. By performing the Corn Dance, with more than one hundred dancers.

Q. What 1956 film, starring Dana Andrews as a cavalry scout, is a tale of the kidnapping of a prominent New Mexican's daughter?

A. *Comanche.*

Q. What Albuquerque native was one of the original Keystone Cops?

A. Slim Summerville.

Q. What 1972 film starring Dean Martin and Rock Hudson was made in Chama and Abiquiu?

A. *Showdown.*

Q. Albuquerque was the location for filming what 1971 movie starring Robert Blake and Ernest Borgnine?

A. *Ripped Off.*

Q. John Lewis of Albuquerque founded what noted musical group?

A. Modern Jazz Quartet.

Q. What two characters were the heroes in the 1946 western *In Old New Mexico*?

A. The Cisco Kid and Pancho.

Q. Who from the *Doogie Howser, M.D.* TV series was born and raised in Albuquerque?

A. Neil Patrick Harris, who played Doogie.

Q. What is the name of the 1964 film, starring Yul Brynner, George Segal, and Pat Hingle, that tells the tale of a Civil War veteran's new confrontations when he returns home to New Mexico?

A. *Invitation to a Gunfighter.*

Q. What 1974 film starring Eddie Albert, Billy Dee Williams, and Frankie Avalon was shot in Santa Fe?

A. *The Take.*

Q. Who from Alamogordo played the mother on TV's *Lassie* during the 1950s?

A. Jan Clayton.

Q. What 1991 film about a New Mexico waitress starred Brooke Adams, Ione Skye, and James Brolin?

A. *Gas Food Lodging.*

Q. What Albuquerque actress has starred in such films as *Urban Cowboy, Funny Farm*, and *Final Approach*?

A. Madolyn Smith.

Q. What animator, famous for stone-age and space-age cartoons, lived in Melrose?

A. William Hanna, of the *Flintstones* and *Jetsons* team of Hanna-Barbera.

Q. Walter Mathau and Alexis Smith starred in what 1978 film about horse racing that was filmed in Ruidoso?

A. *Casey's Shadow.*

Q. Who rescued Fay Wray from King Kong?

A. Bruce Cabot of Carlsbad.

Q. Parts of the 1977 movie *The Sorcerer*, in which Roy Scheider and some comrades drive a truck of explosives through the jungle, were filmed where in the state?

A. Farmington.

Q. What New Mexico native starred in two films of the 1970s that were nominated for a best picture Oscar?

A. Ronny Cox, for *Deliverance* and *Bound for Glory.*

Q. What 1979 movie, filmed at Eaves Ranch and Jemez Springs, picked up the tale of characters played by Paul Newman and Robert Redford in an award-winning 1969 film?

A. *Butch and Sundance, the Early Years.*

Q. Where can you watch a live performance of *The Last Escape of Billy the Kid*?

A. Lincoln, during the Old Lincoln Days Celebration each August.

Q. Where in the state has Bugs Bunny made a wrong turn?

A. Albuquerque.

Q. Clint Eastwood finds himself in the middle of a New Mexico land dispute in what 1972 movie that also stars Robert Duvall and John Saxon?

A. *Joe Kidd.*

Q. What was the first opera performed at the Santa Fe Opera?

A. *Madame Butterfly.*

Q. What 1975 movie starring Gene Hackman, Candice Bergen, James Coburn, and Ben Johnson was filmed in Chama, White Sands, and Taos?

A. *Bite the Bullet.*

Q. Where would you go in April to celebrate Dinosaur Days?

A. Clayton.

Q. What 1983 film, directed by Robert Young, was shot around Santa Fe, Chama, and Las Vegas and has Edward James Olmos fleeing from Texas Rangers?

A. *The Ballad of Gregorio Cortez.*

◆

Q. Where was the 1912 silent movie *The Old Actor*, starring America's Sweetheart Mary Pickford, filmed?

A. Albuquerque.

◆

Q. Mike Judge of Albuquerque created what MTV duo?

A. Beavis and Butt-Head.

◆

Q. What 1976 movie starring Anne Jeffries was filmed at Eaves Ranch?

A. *Southern Doublecross.*

◆

Q. What wacky 1987 movie starring Bette Midler, Shelley Long, and Peter Coyote was filmed in Albuquerque, Cerrillos, and Abiquiu?

A. *Outrageous Fortune.*

◆

Q. What Indian celebration, one of the nation's largest, takes place at Red Rock State Park near Gallup every year?

A. Inter-Tribal Indian Ceremonial.

◆

Q. What 1976 robbery-murder movie starred Marjoe Gortner and Lynda Carter and was filmed in Albuquerque?

A. *Bobbi Jo and the Outlaw.*

Q. *The Knotted Strings* by Jake Page is a fictional work dealing with what New Mexico industry?

A. Motion pictures.

◆

Q. A town in New Mexico is mentioned in what Oscar-winning song performed by Judy Garland?

A. "On the Atchison, Topeka, and Santa Fe."

◆

Q. Actors Roy Rogers, Robert Taylor, Lash LaRue, Audie Murphy, Jack Beutel, Paul Newman, Kris Kristofferson, and Emilio Estevez have all portrayed what legendary New Mexico figure?

A. Billy the Kid.

◆

Q. In what year was the Santa Fe Opera Company founded?

A. 1956.

◆

Q. What 1943 horror film tells the story of killings surrounding a circus in New Mexico?

A. *The Leopard Man.*

◆

Q. Where was actress Kim Stanley born?

A. Tularosa.

◆

Q. What actor was born Jacques Etienne deBujac and starred on TV in *Ellery Queen* during the 1950s?

A. Bruce Cabot of Carlsbad.

Q. What 1968 film starring Clint Eastwood, Inger Stevens, and Ben Johnson was filmed around Las Cruces?

A. *Hang 'Em High.*

———◆———

Q. Parts of what 1989 mini-series were filmed in Santa Fe and Angel Fire?

A. *Lonesome Dove.*

———◆———

Q. In which of his hits does George Strait sing about breaking his leg in Santa Fe?

A. "Amarillo by Morning."

———◆———

Q. A cryogenics experiment interrupts a trip from New Mexico to California in what 1991 movie?

A. *Late for Dinner.*

———◆———

Q. Marshal Sam McCloud of the TV series *McCloud* was on temporary duty in New York City from what New Mexico town?

A. Taos.

———◆———

Q. What 1994 cable-TV movie was about UFOs in New Mexico?

A. *Roswell.*

———◆———

Q. Angie Dickinson and Leslie Nielsen teamed up for what 1971 sci-fi flick about a medical clinic in New Mexico?

A. *The Resurrection of Zachary Wheeler.*

Q. What fictional New Mexico town was the setting for TV's *The Rifleman*?

A. North Fork.

◆

Q. Where was the 1977 movie *Convoy*, starring Kris Kristofferson, Ernest Borgnine, and Ali MacGraw, filmed?

A. In and around Albuquerque.

◆

Q. What is the seating capacity of the Santa Fe Opera House?

A. 1,889, with 150 standing room capacity.

◆

Q. David Warner, Nick Mancuso, Kathryn Harrold, and Strother Martin starred in what 1979 horror film about killing vampire bats in New Mexico?

A. *Nightwing.*

◆

Q. Actor Thomas Gomez received an Academy Award for Best Supporting Actor in what 1947 thriller about blackmail and the mob that was set in New Mexico?

A. *Ride the Pink Horse.*

◆

Q. What Albuquerque actress plays the recurring role of Susan, George Costanza's on-again/off-again girlfriend on TV's *Seinfeld*?

A. Heidi Swedberg.

◆

Q. Where can you celebrate Buzzard's Day in June?

A. Carrizozo.

Q. What 1971 film starring Kirk Douglas and Johnny Cash was filmed in Santa Fe?

A. *A Gunfight.*

Q. What do Helen Hayes, Charles MacArthur, Linda Darnell, Paul Hogan, Peter Hurd, and Henriette Wyeth have in common?

A. They all have had homes in or near San Patricio.

Q. What 1976 film starring David Bowie was filmed in Albuquerque, Madrid, White Sands, and Fenton Hole?

A. *The Man Who Fell to Earth.*

Q. What inventive moviemaker toured New Mexico fourteen years before it became a state?

A. Thomas Alva Edison.

Q. What 1969 movie starring Paul Newman and Robert Redford was filmed principally in Taos and Chama?

A. *Butch Cassidy and the Sundance Kid.*

Q. What is the site for the New Mexico Wine and Chile War Festival?

A. Southern New Mexico Fairgrounds in Las Cruces.

Q. John Wayne played the lead in what 1970 western filmed in Santa Fe that also starred Forrest Tucker and Ben Johnson?

A. *Chisum.*

Q. Jimmy Stewart was particularly fond of what at Albuquerque's La Posada Hotel?

A. The hamburgers.

———◆———

Q. Who is the head of Amblin Entertainment?

A. Steven Spielberg, who has a residence in Santa Fe.

———◆———

Q. Where did director Leslie Fenton find the right location for taking moviegoers through his *Streets of Laredo* in 1948?

A. Gallup.

———◆———

Q. What star of the movies *Clean and Sober* and *Edward Scissorhands* was raised in Albuquerque?

A. Kathy Baker.

———◆———

Q. *Salt of the Earth* is an acclaimed 1953 film about workers in New Mexico who do what kind of work?

A. Mining.

———◆———

Q. The Partridge Family helped a runaway return home to what New Mexico city?

A. Albuquerque.

———◆———

Q. What 1968 western, set in nineteenth-century New Mexico, starred Sean Connery and Brigitte Bardot and was based on a Louis L'Amour novel?

A. *Shaluko.*

Q. What writing duo co-wrote the songs "That'll Be the Day," "Peggy Sue," "It's So Easy to Fall in Love," "Everyday," and "Oh, Boy"?

A. Norman Petty (of Clovis) and Buddy Holly.

◆

Q. Where in the state was the 1970 film *There Was a Crooked Man*, starring Henry Fonda and Kirk Douglas, filmed?

A. Near La Joya.

◆

Q. The 1912 silent film *Pueblo Legend*, starring Mary Pickford, was filmed where in the state?

A. Isleta Pueblo.

◆

Q. What is the state's largest zoo?

A. Rio Grande Zoo in Albuquerque.

◆

Q. What 1969 film starring Glenn Ford and Carolyn Jones was filmed in Santa Fe?

A. *Heaven with a Gun.*

◆

Q. The theft of Billy the Kid's Tombstone (later recovered) inspired what contest in Fort Sumner?

A. The World's Richest Tombstone Race, in which racers carry eighty-pound tombstones through an obstacle course.

◆

Q. What 1946 movie, starring Judy Garland, Ray Bolger, and Angela Lansbury and telling the story of polite, New Mexico-based waitresses, won an Academy Award for best song?

A. *The Harvey Girls.*

Q. What internationally prominent entertainer was born with the last name of Guynes in New Mexico on November 11, 1962?

A. Demi Moore.

———◆———

Q. Parts of what 1974 Chevy Chase movie about TV was filmed in the area around Ghost Ranch?

A. *The Groove Tube.*

———◆———

Q. When was the Santa Fe Chamber Music Festival founded?

A. 1973.

———◆———

Q. What 1994 romantic comedy about speech writers working on a political campaign in New Mexico starred Geena Davis and Michael Keaton?

A. *Speechless.*

———◆———

Q. The Miss Navajo Nation Pageant is part of what event?

A. Shiprock Navajo Fair.

———◆———

Q. What TV movie about a young Pony Express rider starred Leif Garrett and was filmed in large part at San Ildefonso Pueblo and Valley Grande?

A. *Peter Lundy and the Medicine Hat Stallion.*

———◆———

Q. What star of *I Dream of Jeannie* and *The Bob Newhart Show* lives in Albuquerque?

A. Bill Daily.

Q. What 1935 film was Gene Autry's screen debut?

A. *In Old Santa Fe.*

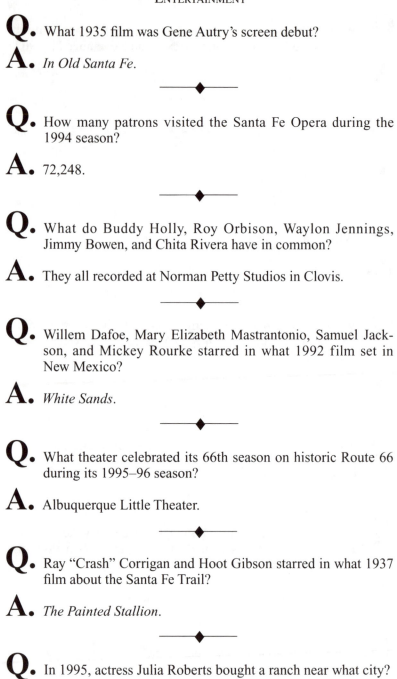

Q. How many patrons visited the Santa Fe Opera during the 1994 season?

A. 72,248.

Q. What do Buddy Holly, Roy Orbison, Waylon Jennings, Jimmy Bowen, and Chita Rivera have in common?

A. They all recorded at Norman Petty Studios in Clovis.

Q. Willem Dafoe, Mary Elizabeth Mastrantonio, Samuel Jackson, and Mickey Rourke starred in what 1992 film set in New Mexico?

A. *White Sands.*

Q. What theater celebrated its 66th season on historic Route 66 during its 1995–96 season?

A. Albuquerque Little Theater.

Q. Ray "Crash" Corrigan and Hoot Gibson starred in what 1937 film about the Santa Fe Trail?

A. *The Painted Stallion.*

Q. In 1995, actress Julia Roberts bought a ranch near what city?

A. Taos.

Q. Who from New Mexico won the Emmy for outstanding supporting actress in a limited series or special in 1985?

A. Kim Stanley, for *Cat on a Hot Tin Roof* ("American Playhouse").

———◆———

Q. In keeping with the tradition of melodrama, the Engine House Theater in Madrid encourages the hissing and booing of the villain by the audience, but allows only what specific objects to be thrown at him?

A. Marshmallows.

———◆———

Q. What city was the location for filming the 1988 remake of *And God Created Woman*, starring Rebecca DeMornay?

A. Santa Fe.

———◆———

Q. *Santa Fe Stampede* stars John Wayne as part of what western film trio?

A. The Three Mesquiteers.

———◆———

Q. Where was the 1970 Larry Hagman-Joan Collins movie *Up in the Cellar* (also called *Three in the Cellar*) filmed?

A. Las Cruces.

———◆———

Q. What town is the home of Ilfeld Auditorium?

A. Las Vegas.

———◆———

Q. John Payne, Faith Domergue, Rod Cameron, and Slim Pickens starred in what 1955 film about a train carrying rifles in New Mexico?

A. *Santa Fe Passage*.

Q. What screen legend's last acting role was a 1978 TV film whose co-stars included members of the casts of *Father Knows Best*, *Star Trek*, *The Brady Bunch*, and *The Partridge Family*?

A. Pecos resident Greer Garson, in *Little Women*.

◆

Q. What 1985 lighthearted western starring Kevin Costner was filmed in Galisteo, Abiquiu, and Santa Ana Pueblo?

A. *Silverado*.

◆

Q. Ronald Reagan, Errol Flynn, Olivia de Havilland, and Raymond Massey were among the stars of what 1940 film set in New Mexico?

A. *Santa Fe Trail*.

◆

Q. What 1984 movie starring Roy Scheider was filmed in part at the Very Large Array on the San Augustin Plains?

A. *2010*.

◆

Q. What show was so popular that the Albuquerque Civic Light Opera Association performed it three years in a row?

A. *Nunsense* (1991–93).

◆

Q. Where was *Covenant with Death*, a 1967 film release starring George Maharis, filmed?

A. Santa Fe.

◆

Q. Audiences went ape over what 1978 movie starring Clint Eastwood that was filmed in Albuquerque, Taos, and Santa Fe?

A. *Every Which Way But Loose*.

Q. Who made up the original Norman Petty Trio, which was based in Clovis, and had a big hit with "Mood Indigo"?

A. Vi and Norman Petty and Jack Vaughn.

———◆———

Q. What 1991 movie starring Billy Crystal had him taking part in a cattle drive through New Mexico?

A. *City Slickers*.

———◆———

Q. Where were parts of *Star Wars* filmed?

A. White Sands.

———◆———

Q. What New Mexico city is mentioned in the song "(Get Your Kicks on) Route 66"?

A. Gallup.

———◆———

Q. What film starring Cesar Romero, Tab Hunter, Divine, and Lainie Kazan was filmed in Santa Fe?

A. *Lust in the Dust*.

———◆———

Q. What Silver City native played Harry Bentley on TV's *The Jeffersons*?

A. Paul Benedict.

———◆———

Q. *The Hallelujah Trail*, a 1965 film starring Burt Lancaster, Martin Landau, Jim Hutton, Brian Keith, Donald Pleasence, and Lee Remick, was shot where in the state?

A. Gallup.

Q. What former Albuquerque resident won an Emmy in 1995?

A. Kathy Baker, for her work on *Picket Fences*.

———◆———

Q. What 1970s drama series starring Anthony Quinn and Mike Farrell was set in Albuquerque?

A. *The Man and the City.*

———◆———

Q. What actress, singer, and variety show legend has a home in Santa Fe?

A. Carol Burnett.

———◆———

Q. What 1972 film release starring Paul Newman, Lee Marvin, and Strother Martin was filmed in Santa Fe and Truchas?

A. *Pocket Money.*

———◆———

Q. Kermit the Frog passes through Albuquerque on his way to Hollywood in what 1979 film?

A. *The Muppet Movie.*

———◆———

Q. In what year did Capitan's Smokey Bear Museum open?

A. 1960.

———◆———

Q. Where was the 1958 Paul Newman movie *The Left-Handed Gun* filmed?

A. Santa Fe.

Q. Luminaria tours take place in Albuquerque on what day?

A. December 24.

◆

Q. What New Mexico mountains provided the rugged terrain for 1981's Charles Bronson/Lee Marvin chase movie *Death Hunt?*

A. Sandia.

◆

Q. *The Man From Laramie*, the 1955 western starring Jimmy Stewart, was filmed not in Laramie but where?

A. Taos Pueblo and Santa Fe.

◆

Q. In what year did the Engine House Theater in Madrid open to the public?

A. 1983.

◆

Q. What was the first radio station to broadcast in the state?

A. KOB in Las Cruces in 1921 (moved to Albuquerque in 1923).

◆

Q. What 1951 B western starring Dane Clark, Ben Johnson, and Peter Graves was filmed in Gallup?

A. *Fort Defiance.*

◆

Q. Where in the state did Jim Morrison of the Doors once live?

A. Albuquerque.

Q. Bette Davis and Ernest Borgnine starred in what 1971 movie filmed in Belen and Los Lunas?

A. *Bunny O'Hare.*

———————◆———————

Q. Maria Benitez of Taos is known for what form of entertainment?

A. Dancing.

———————◆———————

Q. Where was the 1971 movie *Scandalous John,* starring Brian Keith and Harry Morgan, filmed?

A. Alamogordo.

———————◆———————

Q. What Albuquerque native is best known for her portrayal of Myra in *Dr. Quinn, Medicine Woman*?

A. Helene Udy.

———————◆———————

Q. What New Mexico native starred in the movie *Deliverance*?

A. Ronny Cox.

———————◆———————

Q. Where was the 1974 western *Las Cruces,* starring Jim Mitchum, filmed?

A. Radium Springs.

———————◆———————

Q. What New Mexico town hosts the "Trails 'n' Rails" festival each June?

A. Las Vegas.

Q. What New Mexico actress was nominated for a Tony and Drama Desk Award in 1986 for her performance in *The Mystery of Edwin Drood*?

A. Patti Cohenour.

———◆———

Q. What acclaimed 1951 movie starring Kirk Douglas and Jan Sterling was inspired by a true story of a dying miner in a New Mexico cave?

A. *The Big Carnival.*

———◆———

Q. In what year did the state's first television station begin broadcasting?

A. 1948, as NBC affiliate KOB-TV in Albuquerque.

———◆———

Q. What 1969 movie starring Anthony Quinn, Shelley Winters, and Claude Akins was filmed near Chama?

A. *Flap.*

———◆———

Q. What is the state's legal drinking age?

A. Twenty-one years.

———◆———

Q. What late resident of Santa Fe played a rooster and wrote songs for Walt Disney's animated *Robin Hood*, released in 1973?

A. Roger Miller.

———◆———

Q. Where is the New Mexico Chile Cookoff held each October?

A. Ruidoso.

Q. What New Mexico native starred in the 1977 horror film *The Girl Called Hatter Fox*, which was filmed in Santa Fe and Albuquerque?

A. Ronny Cox.

Q. What is the seating capacity of the Albuquerque Little Theater?

A. 570.

Q. Dwight Schultz portrays Robert Oppenheimer in what 1989 film about research at Los Alamos?

A. *Fat Man and Little Boy*.

Q. Bob Dylan and the Bellamy Brothers each had top five hits with songs named for what New Mexico city?

A. Santa Fe.

Q. What New Mexico native's early films included *Choices, Parasite,* and *Young Doctors in Love*?

A. Demi Moore.

Q. What city was home to the Kitchen Opera House at the turn of the century?

A. Gallup.

Q. What 1951 movie about Quantrill's Raiders starred Alan Ladd and John Ireland and was filmed in Gallup?

A. *Red Mountain*.

Q. What 1947 film about a Spanish-American War veteran searching for his father's killers starred Robert Mitchum and Teresa Wright and was filmed in Gallup?

A. *Pursued.*

———◆———

Q. During what June event in Santa Fe do participants carry an ancient statue of the Blessed Virgin Mary from St. Francis Cathedral to Ruidoso Chapel and back?

A. La Conquistadora.

———◆———

Q. What 1981 film starring Klinton Spilsbury, Michael Horse, Christopher Lloyd, and Jason Robards was filmed in Santa Fe?

A. *The Legend of the Lone Ranger.*

———◆———

Q. What was the first FM radio station in Clovis?

A. KTQM, founded in 1963.

———◆———

Q. What natural stone amphitheater is located ten miles south of San Jon?

A. Caprice Amphitheater.

———◆———

Q. Where in the state was the 1970 Roger Corman movie *Gas-s-s-s,* starring Cindy Williams, Bud Cort, Ben Vereen, and Talia Shire, filmed?

A. Albuquerque.

———◆———

Q. What major celebration takes place in Santa Fe on Labor Day?

A. Fiesta de Santa Fe.

Q. In the "Peanuts" comic strip, Snoopy sometimes reminisces about quaffing root beers with what native of New Mexico?

A. Bill Mauldin, cartooning pal of "Peanuts" creator Charles Schulz.

Q. What 1973 movie starring Dina Merrill, Lloyd Bridges, Pat Hingle, and Gilbert Roland was filmed at Ghost Ranch?

A. *Running Wild.*

Q. What annual event takes place in Capitan the first week in July?

A. Smokey Bear Stampede, a celebration that includes races, a rodeo, and a barbecue.

Q. What 1986 song with a New Mexico city in its title was a top forty country single for singer Jim Glaser?

A. "The Lights of Albuquerque."

Q. Where in the state was the 1958 movie *The Nine Lives of Elfrego Baca*, starring Robert Loggia, filmed?

A. Cerrillos.

Q. When is Feast Day celebrated at San Ildefonso Pueblo each year?

A. January 23.

Q. What swinging singer/songwriter worked as a barber in the town of Roy in 1927 before pursuing a full-time career in music?

A. Bob Wills.

HISTORY

C H A P T E R   T H R E E

Q. Who was the first "through" passenger on the Butterfield Overland Stage Company's route through Steins in 1858?

A. Waterman L. Ownby, a reporter for *The New York Herald*.

◆

Q. Who confessed to the killing of legendary sheriff Pat Garrett just east of Las Cruces in 1908?

A. Jesse Wayne Brazel.

◆

Q. The ruins of what dwelling place in New Mexico were known (until 1887) as "the largest apartment house in the world"?

A. The Anasazi city in Chaco Canyon.

◆

Q. Where does the state name "New Mexico" rank in age among the fifty states?

A. Second, after Florida ("New Mexico" is thought to have been first spoken in Spanish in 1565, and first used in print in 1582).

◆

Q. In what year was the city of modern Aztec, the seat of San Juan County, founded?

A. 1890.

Q. When did New Mexico native Smokey Bear become the national symbol of firefighting?

A. June 1950.

———◆———

Q. What notable event happened in the Isleta Pueblo (near Albuquerque) on May 5, 1970?

A. A tribal election granted women the right to vote in tribal matters.

———◆———

Q. Who was the first person legally hanged in Lincoln County?

A. William Wilson in 1875.

———◆———

Q. For whom is the town of Gallup named?

A. David L. Gallup, a paymaster for the Atlantic and Pacific Railroad.

———◆———

Q. What New Mexico congressman met with Saddam Hussein in 1995 to negotiate the release of two Americans who strayed across the Kuwait border into Iraq?

A. Bill Richardson.

———◆———

Q. In what year was Taos founded?

A. 1617.

———◆———

Q. Where is the only fully restored kiva (an ancient underground Indian ceremonial chamber) in the United States?

A. Aztec Ruins National Monument.

Q. Who from Abiquiu founded the state's first co-educational school?

A. Padre Antonio Jose Martinez.

Q. What Navajo war chief headed the first Navajo police?

A. Manuelito.

Q. When was the first permanent colony established by the Spanish in New Mexico?

A. 1598 in San Juan.

Q. What force attacked the town of Columbus during the early morning of March 9, 1916?

A. General Francisco (Pancho) Villa and his army.

Q. When was the first railroad track laid in New Mexico?

A. November 30, 1878.

Q. Bloomfield was home base for what nineteenth-century outlaw group?

A. The Stockton Gang.

Q. What former New Mexico Supreme Court justice was a classmate of U.S. Supreme Court Justice Sandra Day O'Connor at Stanford University Law School?

A. Daniel Sisk.

Q. On what date was New Mexico admitted as a state to the Union?

A. January 6, 1912.

Q. In what year was the Cathedral of St. Francis in Santa Fe built?

A. 1869.

Q. What was the first Indian tribe in the United States to offer tax-exempt municipal bonds to institutional investors?

A. New Mexico's Jicarilla Apache tribe, in 1985 ($30.2 million).

Q. Where does Santa Fe rank in age among U.S. capital cities?

A. First.

Q. Who founded Albuquerque?

A. Colonial Governor Don Francisco Cuervo y Valdes.

Q. After he settled in Santa Fe, famed cowboy detective Charles A. Siringo could be seen riding around town on his white horse named what?

A. Sailor Gray.

Q. What happened at 5:29:45 A.M. on July 16, 1945?

A. First atomic test explosion at the White Sands Missile Range near Alamogordo.

Q. What is the state slogan?

A. Land of Enchantment.

———◆———

Q. What town voted in 1853 to move in order to retain its Mexican citizenship?

A. Mesilla.

———◆———

Q. What location was a childhood home of Gen. Douglas MacArthur?

A. Fort Selden.

———◆———

Q. In what New Mexico town was Conrad Hilton born?

A. San Antonio.

———◆———

Q. What is thought to be the oldest church in America?

A. San Miguel Chapel in Santa Fe.

———◆———

Q. In what year was the brand registered for the legendary Bell Ranch?

A. 1875.

———◆———

Q. For whom is Cannon Air Force Base named?

A. Gen. John K. Cannon, a commander of the Tactical Air Command.

Q. In what year was Albuquerque founded?

A. 1706.

---◆---

Q. Who in New Mexico was also known as Henry Antrim, Henry McCarty, and William Bonney?

A. Billy the Kid.

---◆---

Q. The Treaty of Guadalupe-Hidalgo ended what war?

A. Mexican-American War.

---◆---

Q. What was the first building in Gallup?

A. Blue Goose Saloon, erected circa 1860.

---◆---

Q. What U.S. legislator from New Mexico clarified the correct spelling of "chile" (as opposed to "chili") in the *Congressional Record* in 1983?

A. Senator Pete Domenici.

---◆---

Q. Who designated New Mexico a royal colony of Spain in 1609?

A. King Phillip III.

---◆---

Q. In what year was the University of New Mexico founded?

A. 1889.

Q. What U.S. president once presented ebony canes bearing his signature to nineteen pueblos?

A. Abraham Lincoln.

Q. When was the current New Mexico State capitol built?

A. 1966.

Q. What is the oldest continually occupied dwelling in America?

A. Acoma Pueblo.

Q. Who were the Harvey Girls?

A. Youthful ladies, mostly from the Eastern United States, hired by entrepreneur Fred Harvey to work in his Harvey House restaurants along the Santa Fe Railroad in New Mexico and throughout the West.

Q. As of 1995, who is the youngest man to be elected governor of the state of New Mexico?

A. David E. Cargo (37 years, 11 months); governor from 1967 to 1971.

Q. How many New Mexican residents signed up to join Teddy Roosevelt's Rough Riders at San Juan Hill?

A. 340, about one-third of the total force.

Q. Miguel Trujillo of Isleta Pueblo is probably best known for what?

A. Spearheading the fight to win the right to vote for Native Americans.

Q. For whom was the town of Clayton named?

A. U.S. Senator Stephen Dorsey's son.

———◆———

Q. Hobbs became a boom town when oil was discovered by what venture on November 8, 1928?

A. Midwest Refinery Co. (now known as Amoco). The well began producing seven hundred barrels a day, and today it is still producing oil.

———◆———

Q. Katherine Ortega of Tularosa held what federal position?

A. U.S. Treasurer.

———◆———

Q. When was the Southwestern Indian Polytechnic Institute in Albuquerque officially dedicated?

A. September 16, 1971.

———◆———

Q. Where does the Spanish colony at San Juan rank in age among Spanish colonies in what is now the United States?

A. Second (founded in 1598). St. Augustine, Florida, was founded in 1565.

———◆———

Q. What was the dollar amount of the Gadsden Purchase, which included New Mexico territory?

A. $10 million.

———◆———

Q. The flags of what four nations have flown over the Palace of the Governors in Santa Fe since it was built in 1609?

A. Spain, Mexico, the Confederate States of America, and the United States of America.

Q. What was the Duke of Alburquerque's position in Spanish colonial government?

A. He was a viceroy in Mexico City.

———◆———

Q. What 1983 U.S. Supreme Court case established "Congress' overriding objective of encouraging tribal self-government and economic development" over state laws?

A. *New Mexico v. Mescalero Apache Tribe.*

———◆———

Q. Who was the founding father of Santa Fe?

A. Don Pedro de Peralto.

———◆———

Q. As of 1995, who is the oldest person to be elected governor of New Mexico?

A. Bruce King (66 years, 8 months).

———◆———

Q. In what year was the town of Gallup founded?

A. 1881.

———◆———

Q. Don Francisco Vasquez de Coronado searched southwest New Mexico for what in 1542?

A. The fabled Seven Cities of Cibola (Gold).

———◆———

Q. How many firms in Albuquerque were owned by Native Americans in 1987?

A. 180.

Q. New Mexico's becoming a state brought the number of stars on the U.S. flag to what?

A. Forty-seven.

Q. What was the Long Walk in 1864?

A. The forced march of 8,000 Navajos from Arizona to Fort Sumner, New Mexico.

Q. Who killed Billy the Kid on July 14, 1881?

A. Lincoln County Sheriff Pat Garrett.

Q. When did the Lincoln County War start and end?

A. It started on February 18, 1878, and ended on July 19, 1878.

Q. Where can you see Mimbres Indian homes that were abandoned more than six hundred years ago?

A. Gila Cliff Dwellings, near Silver City.

Q. Who are two famous frontierspeople buried at Kit Carson Park near Taos?

A. Kit Carson and Mabel Dodge Luhan.

Q. What eighteenth-century mission is the oldest U.S. shrine to Our Lady of Guadalupe?

A. Santuario de Guadalupe, in Santa Fe.

Q. Who was the first governor of New Mexico?

A. W. C. McDonald.

Q. Where was the Gadsden Purchase (which made the territory of New Mexico part of the United States) signed?

A. Old Mesilla.

Q. What was New Mexico's first completely oil-surfaced road?

A. Route 66.

Q. How did the city of Albuquerque originally spell its name?

A. Alburquerque, following the spelling of the Duke of Alburquerque.

Q. When was Laguna Pueblo founded?

A. The 1400s.

Q. What was New Mexico outlaw Billy the Kid's first known criminal offense?

A. Stealing several pounds of butter.

Q. What 1973 Supreme Court ruling found that Indians are exempt from state taxation on incomes earned within reservation boundaries?

A. *Mescalero Apache Tribe v. Jones, Commissioner, Board of Revenue of New Mexico, et al.*

Q. Who from New Mexico was Secretary of the Interior under President Bush?

A. Manuel Lujan Jr.

———◆———

Q. Rio Rancho has been inhabited since when?

A. Though Rio Rancho is a relatively new city, an Ice Age campsite dating back ten thousand years has been excavated within the city limits.

———◆———

Q. In 1861, what town served as the western headquarters for the Confederacy?

A. Old Mesilla.

———◆———

Q. Billy the Kid's first known jailing (at age eighteen) was for what offense?

A. Stealing $70 from a merchant in Silver City. (He escaped by climbing up the chimney.)

———◆———

Q. What part did Fort Stanton play in World War II?

A. It was a POW camp for Germans (1941–45).

———◆———

Q. What was the first church between Durango, Mexico, and St. Louis to be designated as a cathedral?

A. Cathedral of St. Francis of Assisi in Santa Fe.

———◆———

Q. For what items could a chile ristra typically be bartered in the eighteenth century?

A. A pair of shoes, two pounds of sugar, or a pound of chocolate.

Q. What was the most important Civil War battle in New Mexico?

A. The Battle of Glorieta Pass (a Union victory).

Q. Who in New Mexico history was called "Cattle King of the Pecos"?

A. John Chisum.

Q. What did the troops of the Thirty-Fourth Infantry Division training at Camp Cody nickname themselves?

A. Sandstorm Division.

Q. In what year did Gallup host its first Inter-Tribal Indian Ceremonial?

A. 1922.

Q. What does the Cross of the Martyrs commemorate?

A. Franciscans killed during Santa Fe's Pueblo Indian Revolt of 1680.

Q. When was Sandoval County's Tyuonyi Pueblo abandoned by ancestors of the Cochiti Indians?

A. Circa 1550.

Q. What was the first railroad to come to New Mexico?

A. The Atchison, Topeka, and Santa Fe.

Q. What New Mexico site did President Reagan declare a national memorial in November 1987?

A. DAV Vietnam Veterans National Memorial in Angel Fire.

Q. When was U.S. Independence Day first officially celebrated in New Mexico?

A. 1831.

Q. How did Black Jack Ketcham, the last of the mounted train robbers, die?

A. He was hanged in Clayton on April 26, 1901.

Q. Why was there a flag-raising in the plaza of Mesilla on November 15, 1854?

A. To confirm the Gadsden Purchase.

Q. Where did the only battle of the Mexican War fought in New Mexico take place?

A. Brazito Battlefield.

Q. Who was murdered on the Oregon Road en route to Las Cruces on February 29, 1908?

A. Pat Garrett.

Q. Near what New Mexico town on the old Butterfield stage route did confidence men pull off the Diamond Swindle of 1872 by salting a nearby mountain with diamonds?

A. Lordsburg.

Q. One of the last Indian attacks occurred in March 1883 when Judge and Mrs. H. C. McComas of Silver City were slain by raiders from what tribe?

A. Chiricahua Apache.

Q. Though Silver City's Santa Rita Copper Mines opened in 1805, the town itself wasn't founded until what year?

A. 1870.

Q. What young lieutenant, who later became a famous general of World War I, was assigned to Fort Bayard in 1886?

A. John J. "Black Jack" Pershing.

Q. In what year did the Bradbury Science Museum open in Los Alamos?

A. 1993.

Q. Who was Pablo Abeita?

A. A governor of Isleta Pueblo.

Q. Who was in charge of the U.S. government's top secret project to design the world's first nuclear weapon?

A. J. Robert Oppenheimer in Los Alamos.

Q. What Taos church is considered to be one of the most splendid examples of Spanish Mission architecture in the world?

A. The Church of Ranchos de Taos.

Q. When was Northern New Mexico State School founded?

A. 1909.

———◆———

Q. Who first reported the archeological finds of the Pajarito Plateau in 1880?

A. Adolf Bandelier.

———◆———

Q. Though Fort Stanton has been an Army base, a U.S. Public Health Service Hospital, and a state Tuberculosis Board Hospital, what is it today?

A. A care facility for the mentally retarded.

———◆———

Q. During what historical event did Billy the Kid kill Sheriff Brady?

A. Lincoln County War.

———◆———

Q. In what year did Los Alamos become a city?

A. 1962.

———◆———

Q. When was the Church of Ranchos de Taos built?

A. 1772.

———◆———

Q. In 1938, Otto Helm and Fritz Strassman made what important discovery in Los Alamos?

A. Nuclear fission.

Q. What Indian chief led his tribe in the McComas Massacre?

A. Chatto.

———◆———

Q. Which side won New Mexico's first major Civil War battle at Valverde Battlefield on February 21, 1862?

A. The Confederates.

———◆———

Q. How long after what would be his last train robbery was famed New Mexico bandit Black Jack Ketcham captured?

A. One day (he was wounded while attempting to rob the train by himself).

———◆———

Q. In what year was the modern town of Fort Sumner founded?

A. 1906.

———◆———

Q. On what 2,000-mile trail passing through New Mexico did more than 250,000 head of cattle travel between 1866 and 1895?

A. Goodnight-Loving Trail.

———◆———

Q. In 1546, Cabeza de Vaca and four companions passed through the area that is now Carlsbad, thereby earning what distinction?

A. They were the first Europeans to visit New Mexico.

———◆———

Q. The Mescalero Apaches were the last Indians in the United States to do what?

A. Lay down their arms in recognition of the United States.

Q. Who built by hand the Mission of St. Joseph on the Mescalero reservation?

A. Father Albert Braun O.F.M. and Native American craftsmen, over the course of twenty years.

Q. What is the date of New Mexico's only battle of the Mexican War?

A. December 25, 1846.

Q. Where was Billy the Kid tried and sentenced to hang before making his famous final escape?

A. Old Mesilla.

Q. In what year was Santa Fe's Cross of the Martyrs dedicated?

A. 1920.

Q. The pueblo at Jemez State Monument dates to what century?

A. Fourteenth.

Q. Who established the first great cattle outfit in the Pecos Valley in 1873?

A. John Chisum.

Q. What ancient culture built the Gila Cliff Dwellings?

A. Mogollon.

Q. What is the oldest existing public building in the United States?

A. The Palace of Governors in Santa Fe.

Q. What was the main issue inciting the Lincoln County War?

A. A dispute over a mercantile monopoly.

Q. What territorial governor of New Mexico had a conference with Billy the Kid in an attempt to get him to lay down his arms in exchange for a pardon?

A. Lew Wallace.

Q. What was Project Y?

A. The secret mission, conducted at Los Alamos, to design the world's first nuclear weapon.

Q. How did U.S. Army Capt. Henry W. Stanton die?

A. In a skirmish with New Mexico's Mescalero Apache Indians.

Q. Five major battles with the last stronghold of Apaches occurred between 1859 and 1881 in what area near Alamogordo?

A. Dog Canyon.

Q. Who from New Mexico was Secretary of the Interior under President Harding?

A. Albert B. Fall.

Q. What well-known Islamic activity center was burned, vandalized, and robbed in 1992?

A. Morada, near Abiquiu.

Q. Who founded the Los Alamos Ranch School?

A. Detroit businessman Ashley Pond, in 1918.

Q. According to legend, how did Starvation Peak get its name?

A. From an incident in which Indians trapped 120 Spanish colonists and then gradually starved them.

Q. In what year was the Capilla de San Antonio in Cinequilla built?

A. 1875.

Q. On what date did Gen. S.W. Kearny raise the American flag in Santa Fe?

A. August 18, 1846.

Q. What was built between A.D. 919 and 1130, once had eight hundred rooms, and is the largest antiquity in North America?

A. Pueblo Bonito.

Q. The pueblo in Pecos had a population of 2,500 in 1540, but what was the population by 1838?

A. Seventeen, who later joined the Jemez tribe.

Q. What was the training site for the famous 200th Coast Artillery, which fought on Bataan and Corregidor in World War II?

A. Camp Maximiliano Luna.

Q. Who were the first settlers in the Red River Valley?

A. Gold seekers in the 1880s.

Q. When was Highlands University in Las Vegas established?

A. 1893.

Q. Where is Billy the Kid buried?

A. A cemetery at Old Fort Sumner.

Q. Billy the Kid and Geronimo were both imprisoned at what federal facility in New Mexico?

A. Fort Union.

Q. What sandstone monolith has been inscribed by more travelers over more centuries than any other site in New Mexico?

A. El Morro (Inscription Rock).

Q. When was the Church of San Felipe de Neri in Albuquerque's Old Town Plaza first opened to worshippers?

A. 1706.

Q. What is the youngest pueblo in New Mexico?

A. Laguna.

———◆———

Q. In what year were the Spanish driven out of Santa Fe because of the Pueblo Indian uprising?

A. 1680.

———◆———

Q. For how many years did Spanish governors rule in the Palace of the Governors in Santa Fe?

A. 212.

———◆———

Q. What village, now a national monument, was founded by and named after the founder of the Boy Scouts?

A. Seton Village, after Ernest Thompson Seton.

———◆———

Q. At what pueblo did Francisco Vasquez Coronado meet the first "friendly" Rio Grande Pueblo Indians in 1540?

A. Isleta.

———◆———

Q. In 1909, petroleum was first produced in New Mexico from a well near what town?

A. Dayton.

———◆———

Q. In what year was the seal of New Mexico designed?

A. 1851.

Q. How many Spanish Mission churches have been established in New Mexico?

A. Eight.

◆

Q. Who led the U.S. Army in the one battle of the Mexican War that was fought in New Mexico?

A. Colonel Doniphas.

◆

Q. Which was founded first, the University of New Mexico or New Mexico State University?

A. New Mexico State University, in 1888 (first by a year).

◆

Q. Who founded the first Spanish settlement and church in New Mexico?

A. Juan de Oñate.

◆

Q. When was New Mexico's constitution adopted?

A. 1911.

◆

Q. In 1955, several million tons of uranium were discovered in what county?

A. What is now Cibola County, but at the time was part of Valencia County.

◆

Q. When was the first English language school founded in New Mexico?

A. 1851 in Santa Fe.

Q. Who made an unauthorized attempt to colonize New Mexico in 1590?

A. Gaspar de Sosa of Spain.

———◆———

Q. What U.S. general supervised the building of Fort Marcy?

A. Stephen W. Kearny.

———◆———

Q. Who was the first governor of the territory of New Mexico?

A. James C. Calhoun in 1851.

———◆———

Q. By what route did Cabeza de Vaca become the first European to enter New Mexico?

A. His ship wrecked on the Texas coast, and he had to travel by land back to Mexico.

———◆———

Q. Where was the first gold lode west of the Mississippi River found?

A. The Ortiz Lode Mine at Sierra del Oro, in 1833.

———◆———

Q. What major engineering project was completed on the Rio Grande in 1916?

A. Elephant Butte Dam.

———◆———

Q. Who was the first Spanish American elected governor of New Mexico since the Great Depression?

A. Jerry Apodaca in 1974.

Q. New Mexico was infested by a record number of what insect in 1985?

A. Grasshopper.

———◆———

Q. What was the first highway in the region of New Mexico?

A. El Camino Real (the King's Highway), established in the late sixteenth century.

———◆———

Q. Who is credited with tracing the Santa Fe Trail in 1821?

A. Capt. William Becktell.

———◆———

Q. What cowboy discovered the Carlsbad Caverns in 1901?

A. Jim White.

———◆———

Q. Where did Butch Cassidy and his "Wild Bunch" live in the 1890s?

A. The WS Ranch near Glenwood, where they were cowhands.

———◆———

Q. What ghost town, formerly a thriving mining community, takes its name from New Mexico's governor from 1712–15?

A. Mogollon.

———◆———

Q. Pat Garrett, Billy the Kid, John Chisum, and Lew Wallace were four of the most famous participants in what New Mexico dispute?

A. Lincoln County War.

Q. What town is home of the Harvey House Museum?

A. Belen.

———◆———

Q. Did New Mexico declare itself Union or Confederate during the Civil War?

A. Confederate, though the territory was captured by the Union to prevent Confederate expansion to California gold fields.

———◆———

Q. What county approved the largest industrial revenue bond ($8 billion) in U.S. history in 1995?

A. Sandoval County, for factory expansion by Intel Corporation.

———◆———

Q. Fray Marcos de Niza reported seeing what on September 2, 1539?

A. The fabled "Seven Cities of Gold."

———◆———

Q. For how many men's deaths is Billy the Kid solely responsible?

A. Four (he helped kill five others)—far from the twenty-one of legend.

———◆———

Q. What were the two main causes of the decline of pueblos south of the Pecos River?

A. Disease and Comanche raids.

———◆———

Q. Who established the Church of San Felipe de Neri in Albuquerque?

A. Don Juan Francisco Cuervo y Valdes.

Q. In 1968, a stretch of what river in New Mexico became the first to be designated "wild and scenic" by the U.S. Congress?

A. Rio Grande.

Q. On what date was the design for the state flag adopted?

A. March 15, 1925.

Q. Who led the first complete expedition on the Santa Fe Trail in 1792?

A. Pedro Vial.

Q. In what year did Carlsbad Caverns become a national park?

A. 1930.

Q. In what year did New Mexico become a province of Mexico rather than Spain?

A. 1821.

Q. Who was Speaker of the New Mexico House of Representatives from 1963–69?

A. Bruce King.

Q. Motorized aircraft and vehicles were used in warfare for the first time in U.S. history during what 1916 military operation led by John Joseph "Black Jack" Pershing?

A. The New Mexico-based Punitive Expedition, an effort to stop raids by Pancho Villa.

Q. What was Taos resident Kit Carson's given name?

A. Christopher.

Q. Ralph Bunche of Albuquerque won a Nobel Peace Prize for what?

A. Negotiating the settlement of the Arab-Israeli War of 1949.

Q. Although the Anasazi Indians were peaceful and traded widely with other native Americans, the Navajo word "Anasazi" has what decidedly unfriendly translation?

A. "Enemies of Our Ancestors," though often diplomatically translated as simply "Ancient Ones."

Q. Where did the "Hermit Monk" Juan Maria Augustiniani live his final days?

A. In la Cueva (the Cave) at the base of the Organ Mountains, where he was found murdered.

Q. What lasting discovery did former slave George McJunkin make near Folsom in the early twentieth century?

A. Large bones, which in 1926 were found to be prehistoric mammoth skeletons with imbedded spearpoints or Folsom Points.

Q. Thousands of drawings, some dating back to 1000 B.C., are found at what site near Albuquerque?

A. The Petroglyphs.

Q. What notorious Colfax County outlaw was known as the corpse-maker?

A. Clay Allison.

Q. What was the state's first incorporated town?

A. Elizabethtown, now a ghost town.

◆

Q. Who established Fort Sumner for the U.S. Army?

A. Brig. Gen. James Carleton.

◆

Q. For whom is the town of Hobbs named?

A. James Hobbs, a local farmer and rancher.

◆

Q. Legend has it that what famous figure worked as a dishwasher for the Stratford Hotel in Lordsburg before starting his best-known career?

A. Billy the Kid.

◆

Q. Who discovered gold in Bear Creek near Piños Altos in 1860?

A. John Birch.

◆

Q. Twelve years after Spain lost Santa Fe to the Indians in the Pueblo Rebellion, the Spanish regained the city under whose military leadership?

A. Gen. Don Diego de Vargas.

◆

Q. Who carved the first inscription on famed New Mexico landmark El Morro in 1605?

A. Juan de Oñate.

Q. When was the town of Bernalillo founded?

A. 1698.

◆

Q. What were the two main uses of wool cloth in colonial New Mexican homes?

A. As flooring and in ceilings to prevent dirt from falling into the home.

◆

Q. Where was Geronimo born?

A. Near the headwaters of the Gila River, circa 1823.

◆

Q. What U.S. Senator from New Mexico was named Secretary of Agriculture during the Truman administration?

A. Clinton P. Anderson.

◆

Q. During the Gold Rush of 1849, travelers used a path through New Mexico that was blazed ten years earlier by whom?

A. Josiah Gregg.

◆

Q. The three-day siege and burning of the McSween House climaxed what event?

A. Lincoln County War.

◆

Q. Native American women used to build their own adobe ovens called what?

A. Hornos.

Q. In what year was a stage line first established between Independence, Missouri, and Santa Fe?

A. 1849.

———◆———

Q. What was the highest military position held by New Mexico pioneer Kit Carson?

A. Brigadier General.

———◆———

Q. In what year was construction of the mission church at Isleta Indian Pueblo completed?

A. 1630.

———◆———

Q. Who supervised the forced four-hundred-mile "Long Walk" by Navajos from Fort Wingate to Fort Sumner in 1864?

A. Kit Carson.

———◆———

Q. The United States completed its continental boundaries with what 1853 pact involving New Mexico?

A. The Gadsden Purchase.

———◆———

Q. Who was the leader of the Stockton gang, a group of nineteenth-century New Mexico outlaws?

A. Ex-sheriff Port Stockton.

———◆———

Q. Immediately following his tenure as territorial governor of New Mexico, Lew Wallace received what U.S. government assignment?

A. Minister to Turkey.

Q. What famous outlaw is buried near the ruins of Old Fort Sumner?

A. William Bonney (Billy the Kid).

———◆———

Q. How many acres of New Mexican territory were included in the Maxwell Land Grant in 1865?

A. 1,714,765.

———◆———

Q. New Mexico's land size was reduced in 1861 to help form what?

A. Colorado Territory.

———◆———

Q. What was the location of the first Spanish capital of New Mexico?

A. The Tewa village of Yugeuningge, christened San Juan de Los Cabelleros.

———◆———

Q. What was the first major trade route to the western United States from the east?

A. Santa Fe Trail.

———◆———

Q. What is New Mexico's largest nongovernmental employer?

A. Furr's Supermarkets.

ARTS & LITERATURE

C H A P T E R F O U R

Q. Who was the New Mexican painter commissioned to paint a portrait of President Lyndon B. Johnson?

A. Peter Hurd.

Q. What is a curanderas in New Mexican folklore?

A. Good witch.

Q. Who wrote the words, "The moment I saw the brilliant, proud morning shine high over the deserts of Santa Fe, something stood still in my soul, and I started to attend."?

A. D. H. Lawrence.

Q. What book, written by a New Mexican, is the only one in history to have editions published by both the Pope and Sears, Roebuck?

A. *Ben-Hur.*

Q. What ghost town in southwest New Mexico shares its name with an English bard?

A. Shakespeare, named for the Shakespeare Mining Company.

Q. What 1958 Will Henry novel is set in Silver City?

A. *The Seven Men at Mimbres Spring.*

---◆---

Q. What 2,094-seat venue is home of the New Mexico Symphony Orchestra and the New Mexico Ballet Company?

A. Popejoy Hall in Albuquerque.

---◆---

Q. Where is Patrick O'Malley's 1961 novel *The Affair of the Red Mosaic* set?

A. Taos.

---◆---

Q. During its peak season, what organization is Santa Fe's second largest nongovernmental employer?

A. Santa Fe Opera (the first is St. Vincent's Hospital).

---◆---

Q. *Semi-Native* is a collection of columns by what Albuquerque journalist?

A. Jim Arnholz, now known as Jim Belshaw.

---◆---

Q. What western novelist, who occasionally used the pseudonym Clay Ringold, drew many of his tales from stories he heard at the Overland Hotel in Albuquerque, which his family owned?

A. Ray Hogan.

---◆---

Q. What Phyllis Whitney novel of 1974 was set in Santa Fe?

A. *The Turquoise Mask.*

Q. The late Taos artist Nicholai Fechin is best known for his works in what medium?

A. Woodcarving.

———◆———

Q. Who wrote the 1968 novel *Welcome to Xanadu*, set in Santa Fe?

A. Nathaniel Benchley.

———◆———

Q. In the world of New Mexico artist Georgia O'Keeffe, who were Jingo and Ingo?

A. Her beloved pet chows.

———◆———

Q. What Albuquerque native wrote such novels as *Wolf Song, Grant of Kingdom*, and *The Conquest of Don Pedro*?

A. Harvey Fergusson.

———◆———

Q. Who painted the murals that decorate the Shuler Theatre in Raton?

A. Manville Chapman.

———◆———

Q. Who wrote the 1956 novel *Morning, Noon, and Night*, which is set in Gallup?

A. Lars Lawrence.

———◆———

Q. Jack Williamson of Portales is best known for his writing in what genre?

A. Science fiction.

Q. Who wrote the 1978 novel *The Hawk and the Dove*, which is set in Taos?

A. Leigh Franklin James.

Q. What is considered to be the largest adobe structure in the United States?

A. Cristo Rey Church in Santa Fe.

Q. What 1968 novel by Richard Bradford is set in Santa Fe?

A. *Red Sky at Morning.*

Q. What Arizona native, a resident of Taos since the 1960s, is known worldwide for his paintings of Navajo women?

A. R. C. Gorman.

Q. What 1966 novel written by Frank Waters takes place in Los Alamos?

A. *The Woman at Otowi Crossing.*

Q. What is the state motto?

A. *Crescit Eundo* (It grows as it goes).

Q. Where is N. Scott Momaday's Pulitzer Prize-winning novel *House Made of Dawn* set?

A. Jemez Pueblo.

Q. Who built Cimarron's Old Mill Museum in 1864?

A. Land baron Lucien Maxwell.

◆

Q. What is the title of New Mexican writer Willa Cather's oldest surviving composition?

A. "Dogs."

◆

Q. Who wrote the 1974 novel *The Milagro Beanfield War*, which is set in the state?

A. John Nichols, a New Mexico resident.

◆

Q. What are Shalakos?

A. Six Zuni gods who bring blessings and goodwill.

◆

Q. Where in the state is *Heading West*, the 1981 novel by Doris Betts, set?

A. Bandelier National Monument.

◆

Q. Who wrote *Murder in the Walls* and *You Don't Need an Enemy*, both of which were set in Santa Fe and published in 1971?

A. Richard M. Stern.

◆

Q. According to New Mexican folklore, is the roadrunner aligned with the forces of good or evil?

A. Good.

Q. Who wrote *The Border Trilogy*, which takes place in New Mexico?

A. Cormac McCarthy.

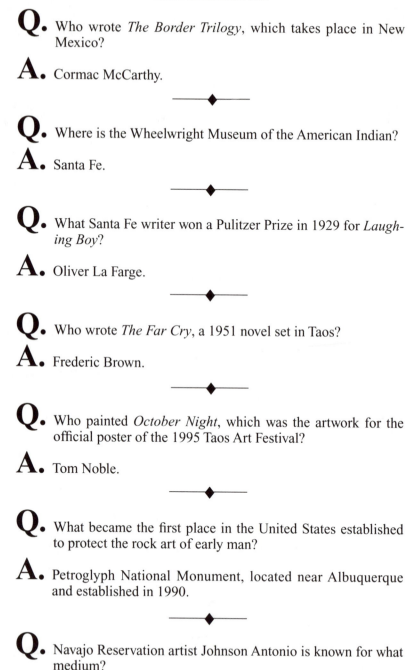

Q. Where is the Wheelwright Museum of the American Indian?

A. Santa Fe.

Q. What Santa Fe writer won a Pulitzer Prize in 1929 for *Laughing Boy*?

A. Oliver La Farge.

Q. Who wrote *The Far Cry*, a 1951 novel set in Taos?

A. Frederic Brown.

Q. Who painted *October Night*, which was the artwork for the official poster of the 1995 Taos Art Festival?

A. Tom Noble.

Q. What became the first place in the United States established to protect the rock art of early man?

A. Petroglyph National Monument, located near Albuquerque and established in 1990.

Q. Navajo Reservation artist Johnson Antonio is known for what medium?

A. Woodcarving.

Q. What New Mexico native wrote the 1921 novel *The Blood of the Conquerers?*

A. Harvey Fergusson.

———◆———

Q. Where is the Vietnam Veterans National Memorial Chapel, the first memorial built to honor Vietnam veterans, located?

A. Near Eagle Nest Lake at Angel Fire, where it was completed in 1971.

———◆———

Q. Who is burned in effigy during the Santa Fe Fiestas each year?

A. Zozobra (Old Man Gloom).

———◆———

Q. Who wrote the 1937 novel *Sea of Grass*, which is set in Datil?

A. Conrad Richter.

———◆———

Q. What famous Santa Fe architect designed many of the Spanish-Pueblo style buildings on the University of New Mexico campus?

A. John Gaw Meem.

———◆———

Q. Who wrote *The Great Taos Bank Robbery?*

A. Tony Hillerman.

———◆———

Q. Who wrote the 1943 novel *The Hills of Home*, which is set in Raton?

A. Curtis Martin.

Q. Who wrote the 1943 novel *Teresita of the Valley*, which is set in the San Luis Valley?

A. Florence C. Means.

───◆───

Q. The former home of what Pulitzer Prize-winning journalist of World War II is now a memorial library in Albuquerque?

A. Ernie Pyle.

───◆───

Q. Who wrote the 1930 novel *Miguel of the Bright Mountain*, which is set in Taos and Santa Fe?

A. Raymond Otis.

───◆───

Q. What are the top three cities in the United States for art sales?

A. Los Angeles, New York City, and Santa Fe (in order).

───◆───

Q. Who wrote *The Common Heart*, which is set in Albuquerque?

A. Paul Horgan.

───◆───

Q. What two sisters from New Mexico wrote the autobiographical book *If Wishes Were Horses* about the education of a veterinarian?

A. Loretta Gage, D.V.M., and Nancy Gage.

───◆───

Q. Where will you find the Morris Miniature Circus?

A. Museum of International Folk Art in Santa Fe.

Q. What former governor of territorial New Mexico wrote a novel that later became an Oscar-winning motion picture?

A. Lew Wallace, author of *Ben-Hur*.

Q. Where is Suzanne Michelle's 1982 novel *Enchanted Desert* set?

A. Santa Fe.

Q. What is the state song?

A. "O Fair New Mexico."

Q. Which people produced the world-famous Saltillo Sarapes between 1750 and 1800?

A. Tlaxcalan Indians, who settled near Saltillo.

Q. Who wrote the 1956 novel *The Royal City*, which is set in Santa Fe?

A. Les Savage Jr.

Q. Simon Ortiz of Acoma Pueblo is known for what category of writing?

A. Poetry.

Q. What 1944 novel by Kyle Crichton takes place in Albuquerque?

A. *The Proud People.*

Q. The prevalent "squash blossoms" design in New Mexican jewelry is not really "squash blossoms" at all but what?

A. Pomegranate blossoms.

———◆———

Q. Where is *No Little Thing*, the 1960 novel by Elizabeth A. Cooper, set?

A. Taos.

———◆———

Q. The design of Loretto Chapel in Santa Fe was inspired by what other famous church?

A. Sainte-Chapelle in Paris.

———◆———

Q. What New Mexico town was the setting for Cleofas M. Jarmillo's 1955 novel *Romance of a Village Girl*?

A. Taos.

———◆———

Q. What is Santa Fe sculptor Glenna Goodacre's most famous work?

A. Memorial for women who served in Vietnam, located in Washington, DC.

———◆———

Q. What 1958 novel by William Eastlake was set in the New Mexico town of Cuba?

A. *The Bronc People.*

———◆———

Q. Who founded the Santa Fe Opera Company?

A. John Crosby.

Q. Who was the first author honored while still alive by the National Cowboy Hall of Fame in its Famous Western Writers category?

A. S(quire) Omar Barker, poet, author, and native of Beulah.

Q. The state capitol is in the shape of what?

A. Zia emblem.

Q. Where was Emerson Blackhorse Mitchell, author of *Miracle Hill: The Story of a Navajo Boy*, born?

A. Near Shiprock.

Q. Who wrote *Trail From Taos*?

A. Loring MacKaye.

Q. What is the name of the New Mexican dude ranch in the novel *Guestward Ho!*?

A. Rancho del Monte.

Q. What Roswell artist married artist Henriette Wyeth?

A. Peter Hurd.

Q. In most European folk tales, witches ride brooms, but in New Mexican folklore, witches ride what?

A. Fireballs.

Q. What is unusual about the Mesa Public Library?

A. It is shaped like a bird.

Q. What 1955 novel by Elizabeth H. Frierwood is set in Artesia?

A. *Candle in the Sun.*

Q. Northeast of Quemado, 400 twenty-foot tall stainless steel poles are part of what work of art?

A. The Lightning Field.

Q. Which short story by John Gregory Betancourt involves a vampire falling in love with a contestant in a beauty pageant?

A. "Miss Vampire New Mexico Meets Her Dream Date."

Q. Who wrote about New Mexico in the 1962 novel *Fire on the Mountain*?

A. Edward Abbey.

Q. The remains of what writer were exhumed from a grave in the Mediterranean, cremated, and then brought to Lobo Mountain?

A. D. H. Lawrence.

Q. What is a bruja in New Mexican folklore?

A. Bad witch.

Q. What New Mexico town did Emerson Hugh use as the setting for his novel *Heart's Desire*?

A. White Oaks.

◆

Q. What Las Cruces native wrote *Children of a Lesser God*?

A. Mark Medoff.

◆

Q. What is unique about the construction of the wooden spiral staircase in Our Lady of Light Church in Santa Fe?

A. It was built without any nails.

◆

Q. What fort was the home base of poet and scout Capt. Jack Crawford?

A. Fort Craig.

◆

Q. What New Mexico artist painted the "Sky Above Clouds" series during the 1960s?

A. Georgia O'Keeffe.

◆

Q. Who wrote the 1959 novel *The Far Mountains*, which is set in Taos?

A. Frank O'Rourke.

◆

Q. Who wrote the 1947 novel *Death in the Claimshack*, which is set in Lincoln County?

A. John Sinclair.

Q. Who wrote the 1971 novel *The Fly on the Wall?*

A. Albuquerque resident Tony Hillerman.

------◆------

Q. What Paul Horgan epic won a Pulitzer Prize and a Bancroft Prize in 1955?

A. *Great River: The Rio Grande in North American History.*

------◆------

Q. What does the New Mexican custom of luminarias symbolize?

A. Lighting the way of the Christ Child.

------◆------

Q. What is the leading handicraft in Chimayo?

A. Weaving.

------◆------

Q. Jemez is the last pueblo where what language is spoken?

A. Tewa.

------◆------

Q. Where does Paul King's 1977 novel *Hermana Sam* take place?

A. Santa Fe.

------◆------

Q. What is the name of the 1980 novel about a University of New Mexico professor who is a vampire?

A. *The Vampire Tapestry.*

Q. Kiowa Ranch, north of Taos, was a home of what noted writer?

A. D. H. Lawrence.

Q. Legend has it that "Black Jack" Ketchum said what as he was about to be hanged in Clayton for train robbery?

A. "Hurry up. I'm due in hell for dinner."

Q. Who wrote, "At midnight drink no water, for I have heard said; that on the strike of midnight; all water goes dead."?

A. Mary Austin, in *Dead Water, New Mexico Legend.*

Q. Who wrote the 1908 novel *The Men of Sapio Ranch*, which is set in Las Vegas, New Mexico?

A. Horace M. DuBose.

Q. What music and poetry event is held near Ruidoso each October?

A. Lincoln County Cowboy Symposium.

Q. How is death portrayed in Northern Hispanic culture?

A. As a female skeleton.

Q. Where does Norman Holes's 1955 novel *The Spider in the Cup* take place?

A. Santa Fe.

Q. Where is the World of Flutes Museum?

A. Truchas.

◆

Q. San Gregorio de Abo mission church, completed in 1651, is one of the few remaining examples in the United States of what style of architecture?

A. Medieval.

◆

Q. Who wrote *My Life on the Frontier, 1864–1882*?

A. Miguel Otero, governor of New Mexico, 1897–1906.

◆

Q. "Brothers 3," a Sherlock Holmes society, meets annually in what New Mexico city?

A. Moriarty.

◆

Q. Where is writer Eugene Manlove Rhodes buried?

A. Rhodes Pass (named for him), high in the San Andres Mountains.

◆

Q. Where was Navajo author Kay Bennett born in 1922?

A. Sheep Springs Trading Point.

◆

Q. In what year did New Mexico's first newspaper, *El Crepusculo de la Libertad* (*The Dawn of Liberty*) begin publication?

A. 1834, in Santa Fe, by Antonio Barrciro.

Q. Where does poet Luci Tapahonso live?

A. Navajo Reservation.

◆

Q. What longtime Taos resident wrote the acclaimed novel *Death Comes to the Archbishop*?

A. Willa Cather.

◆

Q. Why do Navajos place boots of their dead on the wrong feet?

A. To make it hard for evil spirits to follow the departed in the afterlife.

◆

Q. What was New Mexico writer Tony Hillerman's first published novel?

A. *The Blessing Way*, published in 1970.

◆

Q. *Our Lady at the Foot of the Cross Shrine* in Las Cruces is a reproduction of what work of art?

A. Michaelangelo's *Pietà*.

◆

Q. What novel was written at Kiowa Ranch during the author's eleven-month stay there?

A. *St. Mawr*, by D. H. Lawrence.

◆

Q. What pueblo is known for its black-on-black carved pottery?

A. Santa Clara.

Q. The town of Madrid is now an artists community, but before that it was best known for what?

A. Coal mining (and for twenty years it was considered a ghost town).

◆

Q. Ansel Adams immortalized what town in his photo of a full moon rising?

A. Hernandez.

◆

Q. Why are the colors in the state flag red and gold?

A. They are the colors borne by Spanish conquistadors of Queen Isabella of Castile.

◆

Q. What New Mexico native wrote the novel *Bless Me, Ultima*?

A. Rudolfo Anaya.

◆

Q. What Los Lunas object has been theorized to be everything from an ancient form of the Ten Commandments to an inscription by a Greek slave brought to the New World in 500 B.C.?

A. Mystery Stone.

◆

Q. What 1941 novel by Frances Crane is set in Santa Fe?

A. *The Turquoise Shop.*

◆

Q. Where does painter Pablita Velarde live?

A. Santa Clara Pueblo.

Q. Ernest Blumenschein, Bert Phillips, and Joseph Henry Sharp were central to the founding of what lasting organization?

A. Taos Society of Artists.

Q. What do Kachina dolls represent?

A. Kachina dancers, which in turn represent various gods (the dolls themselves never represent the gods).

Q. Who was the model for the main character in the novel *Death Comes to the Archbishop*?

A. Archbishop Lamy of Santa Fe.

Q. Who wrote the 1932 poetic drama *Night Over Taos*, based on the Taos Revolt?

A. Maxwell Anderson.

Q. Who wrote the novel *All the Pretty Horses*, which is set in New Mexico?

A. Cormac McCarthy.

Q. Who wrote, "For a greatness of beauty, I have never experienced anything like New Mexico."?

A. D. H. Lawrence.

Q. Who wrote the state song?

A. Elizabeth Garrett, daughter of legendary sheriff Pat Garrett.

Q. Who wrote the 1900 novel *With Hopes of Steel*, which is set in Las Cruces?

A. Florence F. Kelly.

◆

Q. Who is Doña Peipeiuta?

A. A New Mexican witch who could take her body apart and put it back together again.

◆

Q. Who writes the "One of Our Fifty Is Missing" feature for *New Mexico Magazine*?

A. Richard C. Sandoval.

◆

Q. Who is the protagonist in New Mexican Tony Hillerman's *Coyote Waits, People of Darkness*, and *A Thief of Time*?

A. Jim Chee.

◆

Q. Where is the D. H. Lawrence Ranch and Shrine?

A. San Cristobal.

◆

Q. What former librarian for the New Mexico Military Institute won a Pulitzer Prize in 1955?

A. Paul Horgan.

◆

Q. Who painted the murals at Albuquerque's KiMo Theatre?

A. Karl Von Hassler.

Q. What novel by Cornelia J. Cannon was published in 1934 and is set in Santa Fe?

A. *The Fight for the Pueblo.*

———◆———

Q. What 1995 detective novel by A. J. Holt is set in New Mexico?

A. *Watch Me.*

———◆———

Q. Artists Jozef Bakos, Walter Mruk, Will Shuster, Willard Nash, and Fremont Ellis dubbed themselves what?

A. Los Cinco Pintores (the five painters).

———◆———

Q. *Earth Horizon* is the autobiography of what longtime New Mexico resident?

A. Mary Austin.

———◆———

Q. Who penned the words, "Elsewhere the sky is the roof of the world, but here the earth was the floor of the sky."?

A. Willa Cather, in *Death Comes to the Archbishop*, which is set in Santa Fe.

———◆———

Q. What Acoma Pueblo poet is the author of *From Sand Creek*?

A. Simon Ortiz.

———◆———

Q. What 1944 novel by Robert Bright is set in Taos?

A. *The Life and Death of Little Jo.*

Q. What ranch now includes Rancho de los Burros, a home of the late Georgia O'Keeffe?

A. Ghost Ranch.

Q. Where in New Mexico was Sarah A. Nassour's 1938 novel *Skin of the Gods* set?

A. Jemez Pueblo.

Q. What Albuquerque resident and novelist is a former executive editor of the *New Mexican* newspaper?

A. Tony Hillerman.

Q. Who painted *Jawbone and Fungus* in 1930?

A. New Mexico artist Georgia O'Keeffe.

Q. What Sandra Brown novel, set in New Mexico, was a *New York Times* paperback best seller for two weeks in 1995?

A. *Eloquent Silence.*

Q. Who won a Pulitzer Prize for the biography *Lamy of Santa Fe*?

A. Paul Horgan.

Q. Who wrote *The Vampire Tapestry*, which is set in New Mexico?

A. Suzy McKee Charras.

Q. What 1936 novel by Anna R. Burr is set in Santa Fe?

A. *Golden Quicksand.*

———◆———

Q. Eugene Manlove Rhodes spent the early years of his life in what area of New Mexico that was also the setting for many of his stories?

A. The Tularosa Valley and Southern New Mexico.

———◆———

Q. Who is Doña Sebastiana?

A. The traditional personification of death in Hispanic culture.

———◆———

Q. What was historian Sally Noe referring to in the following passage: "The paved slash that by 1920 drew the adventurer, by 1924 enticed the traveler, and by 1926 beckoned as no other path to distant dreams."?

A. Route 66.

———◆———

Q. Patrick Dennis, best known for *Auntie Mame*, collaborated with Barbara Hooton on what novel about a dude ranch in New Mexico?

A. *Guestward Ho!*

———◆———

Q. For what craft are the residents of Jemez Pueblo most noted?

A. Their distinctive basket weaving.

———◆———

Q. What 1923 novel by Edwin L. Sabin is set in Santa Fe?

A. *The Rose of Santa Fe.*

Q. Indian legend holds that what mountain is named for two young lovers?

A. Tucumcari, after Tocom and Kari.

———◆———

Q. Where in New Mexico does Cornelius Kuipers's 1934 novel *Chant of the Night* take place?

A. Zuni.

———◆———

Q. What is unusual about the architecture of the restored KiMo Theater in Albuquerque?

A. It is Pueblo-art deco, built in 1927.

———◆———

Q. *The Man Who Killed the Deer*, a novel by Frank Waters that is set in Taos, has been in print since it was first published in what year?

A. 1942.

———◆———

Q. In what year was *The Albuquerque Tribune* founded?

A. 1933.

———◆———

Q. What is the state's largest professional arts organization?

A. The New Mexico Symphony Orchestra.

———◆———

Q. Where in New Mexico is the setting for the 1943 novel *In Time of Harvest* by John Sinclair?

A. Willard.

Q. What is the one Sherlock Holmes tale by Sir Arthur Conan Doyle that makes reference to New Mexico?

A. "The Noble Bachelor."

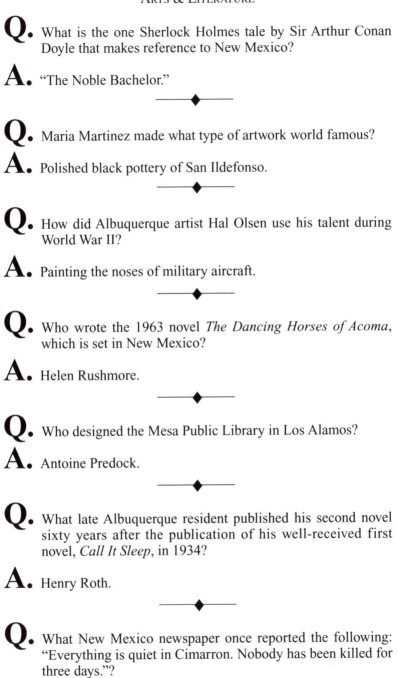

Q. Maria Martinez made what type of artwork world famous?

A. Polished black pottery of San Ildefonso.

Q. How did Albuquerque artist Hal Olsen use his talent during World War II?

A. Painting the noses of military aircraft.

Q. Who wrote the 1963 novel *The Dancing Horses of Acoma*, which is set in New Mexico?

A. Helen Rushmore.

Q. Who designed the Mesa Public Library in Los Alamos?

A. Antoine Predock.

Q. What late Albuquerque resident published his second novel sixty years after the publication of his well-received first novel, *Call It Sleep*, in 1934?

A. Henry Roth.

Q. What New Mexico newspaper once reported the following: "Everything is quiet in Cimarron. Nobody has been killed for three days."?

A. *The Las Vegas Gazette.*

Q. What late resident of Santa Fe wrote lyrics and music for *Big River: The Adventures of Huckleberry Finn* (winner of seven Tony Awards in 1985, including Best Musical)?

A. Roger Miller.

———◆———

Q. What author who was born in Las Vegas, New Mexico, in 1896 wrote such children's books as *Secret of the Andes* and *Blue Canyon Horse*?

A. Ann Nolan Clark.

———◆———

Q. What artist and longtime New Mexico resident was married to photographer Alfred Stieglitz?

A. Georgia O'Keeffe.

———◆———

Q. What New Mexico newspaper has the largest circulation?

A. *The Albuquerque Journal* (about 120,000 daily copies; close to 160,000 on Sundays).

———◆———

Q. What do the murals at the KiMo Theatre in Albuquerque depict?

A. The Seven Cities of Cibola.

———◆———

Q. Who wrote the 1947 book *Albuquerque*?

A. Erna Fergusson.

———◆———

Q. What Santa Fe publishing company bears the name of a legendary naturalist and writer?

A. John Muir Publications.

Q. What are the main four materials used to make Zuni jewelry?

A. Silver, turquoise, mother of pearl, and coral.

◆

Q. What is home of the largest library system in the state?

A. The University of New Mexico, with more than two million books.

◆

Q. What museum along the Turquoise Trail has walls with more than 40,000 bottles incorporated into them, plus more than 20,000 miniatures on display?

A. Tinkertown Museum.

◆

Q. Who wrote the novel *Fair God*?

A. Lew Wallace, territorial governor of New Mexico.

◆

Q. What is the Navajo legend behind the name for Winged Rock?

A. The rock sprouted wings and flew early Navajos to safety when they were attacked by another tribe.

◆

Q. What is the most common design in Saltillo Sarapes?

A. A central Saltillo Diamond.

◆

Q. What Boston art patron moved to Taos in the 1920s and hosted such guests as Thomas Wolfe, Aldous Huxley, D. H. Lawrence, and Willa Cather?

A. Mabel Dodge Luhan.

Q. What famous Chicago high-rise did Nathaniel Alexander Owings, a late resident of Jacoma, design?

A. Sears Tower.

———————◆———————

Q. Who edited *The Spell of New Mexico*, which was published by the University of New Mexico Press in 1984?

A. Tony Hillerman.

———————◆———————

Q. What longtime Albuquerque resident and Golden Spur Award winner has written such books as *Chapultepec*, *Passage to Quivera*, *Rage in Chupadera,* and *Riders to Cibola*?

A. Norman Zollinger.

———————◆———————

Q. What city hosts the annual Southeastern New Mexico Arts and Crafts Festival the first weekend in November?

A. Lovington.

———————◆———————

Q. What New Mexico native has won two Pulitzer Prizes for his political cartooning and is known for his depiction of soldiers "Willy and Joe"?

A. Bill Mauldin.

———————◆———————

Q. What town is home of the famed Millicent Rogers Museum?

A. Taos.

———————◆———————

Q. What late writer who resided in New Mexico wrote the words, "I like trees because they seem more resigned to the way they have to live than other things do."?

A. Willa Cather, in *O Pioneers!*

Q. Who founded the Museum of International Folk Art in 1953 in Santa Fe?

A. Florence Dibell Bartlett.

———◆———

Q. What Santa Fe resident wrote *Caballeros* and *The Wind Leaves No Shadow*?

A. Ruth Laughlin.

———◆———

Q. What is the state poem?

A. *A Nuevo Mexico.*

———◆———

Q. According to the 1990 Census, where does New Mexico rank among the fifty states for the percentage of its residents who speak Spanish as a first language?

A. First (more than thirty-five percent).

———◆———

Q. For what craft is the town of Cordova best known?

A. Woodcarving.

———◆———

Q. What town in the state is named after the writer who penned the words, "If a man does not keep pace with his companions, perhaps it is because he hears a different drummer."?

A. Thoreau (pronounced "through" by locals).

———◆———

Q. *From the Faraway Nearby* is a 1937 painting by what New Mexico artist?

A. Georgia O'Keeffe.

Q. In what city was actress Demi Moore born?

A. Roswell.

———◆———

Q. Where was *The Milagro Beanfield War* filmed?

A. Santa Fe and Truchas.

———◆———

Q. What city was the setting for the 1970s TV detective show *Nakia*, which starred Robert Forster and Arthur Kennedy?

A. Albuquerque.

SPORTS & LEISURE

C H A P T E R   F I V E

Q. What Albuquerque Sports Hall of Famer was the subject for the 1979 made-for-TV movie *A Shining Season*?

A. Olympic miler John Baker.

———◆———

Q. Where will you find the Museum of the Horse?

A. Ruidoso Downs.

———◆———

Q. What nationally recognized University of New Mexico athletic trainer established a renowned student trainers program at the university?

A. Tow Diehm.

———◆———

Q. Who holds the record at New Mexico State University for the most "kills" in a season for the women's volleyball team?

A. Jonna Steffens with 499 in 1990.

———◆———

Q. What town hosts the Great American Duck Race each August?

A. Deming (at Duck Downs on the Southwestern New Mexico Fairgrounds).

Q. For how many years was University of New Mexico football player Mannie Foster a First Team All-Southwest lineman?

A. Three.

—◆—

Q. What Hall of Fame golfer raised in New Mexico was the first player to win $1 million on the LPGA Tour?

A. Kathy Whitworth.

—◆—

Q. Who from New Mexico shares the record of qualifying for the National Finals Rodeo the most times?

A. Olin Young, tied at twenty-six times with Larry Mahan.

—◆—

Q. What Albuquerque Golden Gloves pioneer became a nationally prominent ring official?

A. Jim Cleary.

—◆—

Q. What are New Mexico State University's school colors?

A. Crimson and white.

—◆—

Q. What former University of New Mexico football coach has led the Buffalo Bills to several Super Bowls during the 1990s?

A. Marv Levy.

—◆—

Q. Who is the only Indy Class driver to win three "500" races in one season?

A. Albuquerque native Al Unser Sr.

Q. NBA star Steve Colter played college basketball for what New Mexico school?

A. New Mexico State University.

Q. What was University of New Mexico runner Adolph Plummer's world record time in the 440 dash during the All-WAC meet in May 1963?

A. 44.9 seconds.

Q. How much does a state fishing license cost for a child under age twelve?

A. Nothing.

Q. What was the name of the first manned balloon to make a trans-Atlantic flight?

A. Double Eagle II, with two crew members from Albuquerque.

Q. What NCAA track coach of the year (1967) produced more than ten All-Americans during his tenure at the University of New Mexico?

A. Hugh Hackett.

Q. What New Mexico native holds the record for the most successive wins on the LPGA Tour?

A. Nancy Lopez won all five events she entered in May and June 1978.

Q. Ty Murray of Hobbs has won multiple national championships in what sport?

A. Professional rodeo.

Q. What member of the PGA Tour who has more than a million dollars in career earnings played collegiate golf at New Mexico State University?

A. Tom Byrum.

Q. Where was champion rodeo roper Roy Cooper born?

A. Hobbs, November 13, 1955.

Q. What University of New Mexico runner was the founder of the famed Duke City Dashers track club?

A. John Baker.

Q. Where will you find the golf course rated both by *Golf Digest* in 1984 and by *Golf Week* in 1992 and 1993 as the best public golf course in the United States?

A. Cochiti Lake.

Q. Henri Lambert, chef for Abraham Lincoln, Gen. U.S. Grant, and Napoleon, built what famous hotel in Cimarron?

A. St. James Hotel, founded in 1873.

Q. Santa Rita native Ralph Kiner led the National League in home runs how many seasons in a row?

A. Seven (1946–52).

Q. Angel Fire hosts what tool event in February?

A. World Shovel Race Championships.

Q. What University of New Mexico basketball guard from 1953 to 1956 scored 967 points in his career (45 in one game)?

A. Toby Roybal.

Q. What is the only hotel in the state to be routinely listed among the Top 100 in the United States?

A. The Lodge at Cloudcroft.

Q. What New Mexico native played for the Pirates, Indians, and Cubs and was inducted into the Baseball Hall of Fame in 1975?

A. Ralph Kiner.

Q. What national pro rodeo event is held annually as part of the New Mexico State Fair?

A. All-American Pro Rodeo.

Q. Who from New Mexico was cited by *Sports Illustrated* as one of the Top 20 athletes in the United States for the period 1956–73?

A. Bobby Unser.

Q. How long is the Tour de Los Alamos bike race?

A. Twenty-seven miles.

Q. What is the name of New Mexico State University's football stadium?

A. Chile Bowl.

Q. In the late nineteenth century, Doc Holliday owned a saloon and gambling parlor in what New Mexico town?

A. Las Vegas.

Q. What is the state's most-attended spectator sport?

A. Horse racing.

Q. Who from New Mexico won the 1992 Olympic gold medal in the Men's Parallel Bar competition?

A. Trent Dimas.

Q. Whose ducks have waddled their way to victory in New Mexico's Great American Duck Race more times than anyone else's ducks?

A. Robert Duck.

Q. How many medals were won at the 1992 Summer Olympics by swimmers who trained at the Larry R. Walkup Aquatic Center in Los Alamos?

A. Eleven (four gold and seven bronze).

Q. What basketball star led the University of New Mexico to the 1977–78 WAC crown and a No. 4 national ranking before going on to a celebrated career with the Los Angeles Lakers?

A. Michael Cooper.

Q. What is the world's most photographed event?

A. Kodak Albuquerque International Balloon Fiesta (an estimated twenty-five million photographs were taken in 1994).

Q. For what college did Major League star Mark Acre play baseball?

A. New Mexico State University.

———◆———

Q. What coach introduced wrestling into Albuquerque public schools in 1947?

A. Jack Rushing.

———◆———

Q. What town is home of the La Mesa Race Track?

A. Raton.

———◆———

Q. Who was women's golf coach of the year in the Big West Conference for the 1994–95 season?

A. Jackie Booth of New Mexico State University.

———◆———

Q. What is New Mexico's biggest ski race?

A. Chama Chile Classic.

———◆———

Q. Harvey House restaurants were famous for their pies and cakes along the routes of what railroad?

A. Santa Fe Railroad.

———◆———

Q. Who received the 1983 National Coaches Distinguished Service Award?

A. Dave Tomlinson of Albuquerque.

Q. According to an old law in Albuquerque, how long after your arrival in town do you have to "check all shooting irons" at the local police station?

A. Thirty minutes.

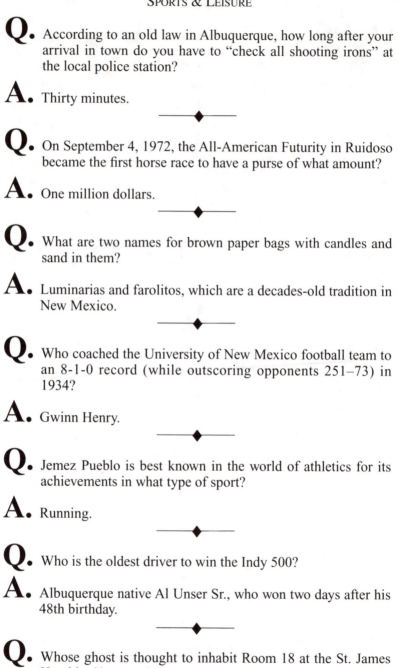

Q. On September 4, 1972, the All-American Futurity in Ruidoso became the first horse race to have a purse of what amount?

A. One million dollars.

Q. What are two names for brown paper bags with candles and sand in them?

A. Luminarias and farolitos, which are a decades-old tradition in New Mexico.

Q. Who coached the University of New Mexico football team to an 8-1-0 record (while outscoring opponents 251–73) in 1934?

A. Gwinn Henry.

Q. Jemez Pueblo is best known in the world of athletics for its achievements in what type of sport?

A. Running.

Q. Who is the oldest driver to win the Indy 500?

A. Albuquerque native Al Unser Sr., who won two days after his 48th birthday.

Q. Whose ghost is thought to inhabit Room 18 at the St. James Hotel in Cimarron?

A. James Wright, killed in a poker game.

Q. What normal sightseeing activity is often restricted in pueblos?

A. Photography.

◆

Q. On March 6, 1966, in Albuquerque, Bob Seagren accomplished what feat?

A. The first indoor pole vault over seventeen feet.

◆

Q. Elephant Butte Lake is renowned for sportfishing for what kind of fish?

A. Black bass.

◆

Q. What 7-foot-3-inch former University of New Mexico center from Australia went on to play pro basketball for the Minnesota Timberwolves and the Chicago Bulls?

A. Luc Longley.

◆

Q. What San Antonio restaurant claims to have the world's best hamburger?

A. Owl Bar & Cafe.

◆

Q. The population of the town of Bernalillo grows from 6,000 to 36,000 during what Labor Day celebration?

A. New Mexico Wine Festival.

◆

Q. What is the nickname used by women's athletic programs at New Mexico State University?

A. Roadrunners.

Q. What race follows a course from Deming to Columbus and back?

A. Great American Bicycle Race.

———◆———

Q. What county is home to more rodeo champions than any other county in the United States?

A. Lea County.

———◆———

Q. What is the nickname of the University of New Mexico's 17,121-seat basketball arena?

A. The Pit.

———◆———

Q. How long is the state's Great American Duck Race?

A. 136 feet.

———◆———

Q. What football star from Albuquerque's Eldorado High School went on to play for the Los Angeles Rams and New Orleans Saints?

A. Jim Everett.

———◆———

Q. Where are Paul Bunyan Days held at the end of August every year?

A. Angel Fire.

———◆———

Q. Why is Shiprock not a haven for rock climbers?

A. Because the Navajos consider the rock sacred and forbid its being climbed.

Q. What is the Elfego Baca Shoot?

A. Part of the Conrad Hilton Golf Tournament, it is a one-hole event covering five miles. Par is fifty.

Q. In what year did Albuquerque Sports Stadium open?

A. 1969.

Q. What New Mexico residence had a rose garden spelling out "Helen," the name of the owner's wife?

A. Dorsey Mansion, the home of U.S. Senator Stephen Dorsey, built in 1878.

Q. Attendance at University of New Mexico basketball games rose to among the top five in the nation under what head coach?

A. Bob King.

Q. With a Railroad Eclipse, a Samson, and a Currie in his collection, what does Portales resident Bill Dalley collect?

A. Windmills.

Q. Farmington hosts what national baseball event every August?

A. Connie Mack World Series Baseball Tournament.

Q. Maxie Anderson and Ben Abruzzo, both of Albuquerque, were part of what ballooning first in August 1978?

A. The first manned trans-Atlantic balloon flight.

Q. Who was honored by the University of New Mexico with the retirement of football jersey No. 42?

A. Bob Santiago, All-American halfback.

———◆———

Q. What group operates Ski Apache Resort?

A. Mescalero Apache Indian Tribe.

———◆———

Q. Who from New Mexico was a McDonald's All-America National All-Star head basketball coach in 1988?

A. Jim Hulsman of Albuquerque High School.

———◆———

Q. In what year did New Mexico native Conrad Hilton found his hotel company?

A. 1919, by renting rooms in his family's home in San Antonio, New Mexico.

———◆———

Q. Who opened the first sporting goods store in the state?

A. H. I. (Iggy) Mulcahy, in Albuquerque.

———◆———

Q. What is the longest and highest narrow-gauge steam railroad in North America?

A. Cumbres and Toltec Scenic Railroad.

———◆———

Q. What coach of football, basketball, track, and baseball at Albuquerque's Menaul High School led teams to victories in more than 1,200 games or meets?

A. Dave Tomlinson.

Q. What are the state's two most popular rivers for rafting?

A. Rio Grande and Rio Chama.

Q. In what community will you find the Shootout at Fryes Old Town?

A. Red River.

Q. What 1962 All-WAC basketball center at the University of New Mexico scored 1,016 points and got 636 rebounds in his career?

A. Ira Harge.

Q. What is the name of the Los Alamos mountain bike club?

A. Tuff Riders.

Q. Who was named minor league baseball's Writer of the Year in 1969?

A. Carlos Salazar of *The Albuquerque Tribune*.

Q. What locale calls itself the "ski town of the Southwest"?

A. Red River.

Q. Why did the University of New Mexico football team make history in 1929 when it traveled to Los Angeles for a game against Occidental College?

A. It was the first time a college team ever flew to an intercollegiate game.

Q. Every summer, some 20,000 Boy Scouts from around the world are hosted where?

A. Philmont Scout Ranch in Cimarron.

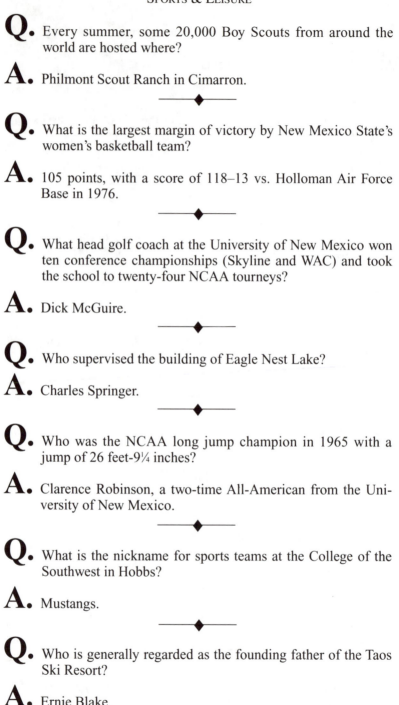

Q. What is the largest margin of victory by New Mexico State's women's basketball team?

A. 105 points, with a score of 118–13 vs. Holloman Air Force Base in 1976.

Q. What head golf coach at the University of New Mexico won ten conference championships (Skyline and WAC) and took the school to twenty-four NCAA tourneys?

A. Dick McGuire.

Q. Who supervised the building of Eagle Nest Lake?

A. Charles Springer.

Q. Who was the NCAA long jump champion in 1965 with a jump of 26 feet-9¼ inches?

A. Clarence Robinson, a two-time All-American from the University of New Mexico.

Q. What is the nickname for sports teams at the College of the Southwest in Hobbs?

A. Mustangs.

Q. Who is generally regarded as the founding father of the Taos Ski Resort?

A. Ernie Blake.

Q. What University of New Mexico football and basketball star coached at Carlsbad High School from 1943 to 1967?

A. Ralph Bowyer.

———◆———

Q. What town is home of the world famous Blue Swallow Motel?

A. Tucumcari.

———◆———

Q. Where is the quarter horse race with the world's richest purse held?

A. Ruidoso Downs, on Labor Day.

———◆———

Q. What is distinctive about Paul (Babe) Parenti's forty-year coaching career at St. Mary's School in Albuquerque?

A. Coaching football, basketball, and baseball, he was the only head coach.

———◆———

Q. What is the state's most renowned spot for freshwater scuba diving?

A. Blue Hole, an artesian well near Santa Rosa.

———◆———

Q. What former University of New Mexico and Dallas Cowboys football star is in the Texas Stadium Hall of Fame?

A. Don Perkins.

———◆———

Q. What club sponsors the state's oldest sanctioned bicycle race?

A. Roadrunners Cycling Club.

Q. What is the common name for the type of customized vintage car that sits close to the ground and is often a focal point of leisure activity in the state?

A. Low-rider.

◆

Q. How long is the Cumbres and Toltec Scenic Railroad?

A. Sixty-four miles.

◆

Q. How many people usually compete each year in the Tour de Los Alamos?

A. More than four hundred.

◆

Q. How many times has Albuquerque race car driver Bobby Unser been the National Points champion?

A. Two.

◆

Q. In what year was Route 66, which crosses New Mexico, decommissioned as a federal highway?

A. 1985.

◆

Q. What University of New Mexico running back great, from 1925 to 1929, was the university's business manager and assistant athletic director from 1965 to 1972?

A. John Dozadelli.

◆

Q. What were the Clovis Meteors?

A. A pioneering New Mexico baseball team of the early twentieth century.

Q. What is the state cookie?

A. Bizcochito.

Q. What Albuquerque resident has hubcaps imbedded in the wall around his yard, plus a piece of wall from the Indy 500 in his yard?

A. Al Unser Jr.

Q. Who founded the Albuquerque International Balloon Fiesta?

A. Sid Cutter.

Q. What lake is the site of the annual Great Milk Carton Boat Race?

A. Lake Van, near Dexter.

Q. Where did Annie Oakley join Buffalo Bill Cody's Wild West Show?

A. St. James Hotel, Cimarron.

Q. The Albuquerque Dukes are a minor league farm team for what Major League franchise?

A. The Dodgers.

Q. How many times has Albuquerque's Bobby Unser won the Indy 500?

A. Three (1968, 1975, and 1981).

Q. What are the three jewels of the Quarter Horse Triple Crown—all held at Ruidoso Downs?

A. Kansas Futurity, Rainbow Futurity, and All-American Futurity.

Q. Until recently, Central Avenue in Albuquerque was also known by what other name?

A. Route 66.

Q. Betty Grable, Lee Marvin, John Wayne, Ronald Reagan, and Burt Lancaster all have slept where in Gallup?

A. El Rancho Hotel.

Q. What team won the Big West regular season title in men's basketball for the 1992–93 season?

A. New Mexico State University.

Q. What reptilian event is held annually on July 4 in Lovington?

A. World's Greatest Lizard Race.

Q. What is New Mexico's equivalent of Colonial Williamsburg?

A. El Rancho de las Golondrinas, a Spanish Colonial living museum.

Q. What University of New Mexico football star has played for the New York Jets and Atlanta Falcons?

A. Terence Mathis.

Q. Where in Las Vegas did Jesse James and Billy the Kid often relax?

A. Montezuma Hot Springs.

Q. Who was the National Turf Writer of the Year in 1979?

A. Carlos Salazar of *The Albuquerque Tribune*.

Q. A New Mexico Supreme Court ruling issued on May 15, 1912, paved the way for allowing what sport to be played on Sundays in the state?

A. Baseball.

Q. Who was the first man to hit fifty home runs twice in the National League?

A. Ralph Kiner of Santa Rita.

Q. What four main ingredients are used in virtually all Southwestern dishes?

A. Tortilla, pinto bean, cheese, and chile.

Q. Who from Albuquerque became the World Light Heavyweight boxing champ in 1974?

A. Bob Foster.

Q. Who earned eight letters at the University of New Mexico in basketball, track, and football from 1925 to 1927 and also pioneered sports officiating in the state by logging more than 2,000 high school and college games?

A. H. I. (Iggy) Mulcahy.

Q. How many WAC titles did the University of New Mexico's gymnastics team win under coach Rusty Mitchell?

A. Eighteen.

Q. Where is the Ned Houk Motorsports Complex?

A. Clovis.

Q. What hotel has a ghost named Rebecca and a mahogany bar once used by Al Capone, and has had Pancho Villa and Judy Garland as guests?

A. The Lodge at Cloudcroft.

Q. In what year did the Los Alamos Mountaineers Club become active?

A. 1952.

Q. Where is the highest golf course in the state?

A. Cloudcroft.

Q. For what pro football team did Farmington's Ralph Neely play?

A. Dallas Cowboys.

Q. How many times has New Mexico's Bobby Unser won the Pike's Peak auto race?

A. Thirteen.

Q. The Albuquerque Dukes have been a member of what baseball league since 1972?

A. Pacific Coast League.

◆

Q. For whom is the basketball court at the University of New Mexico's arena named?

A. Bob King (Bob King Court).

◆

Q. How many of the famous Harvey House restaurants were in New Mexico?

A. Sixteen.

◆

Q. Who is the all-time leader in men's basketball at New Mexico State University in the categories of most points scored, most blocked shots, and most minutes played in a career?

A. Albert "Slab" Jones.

◆

Q. What venue hosted the 1983 NCAA Final Four?

A. University Arena in Albuquerque.

◆

Q. The Smokey Bear Burger is served at the Smokey Bear Restaurant in the Smokey Bear Motel in what town?

A. Capitan.

◆

Q. How long is the Sandia Peak Tramway?

A. 2.7 miles.

Q. Who from Albuquerque has been the announcer of the National Finals Rodeo more times than anyone else?

A. Jay Harwood.

Q. Where is the Roosevelt Rough Riders and Cowboy Reunion held in early August each year?

A. Las Vegas.

Q. What is the name of New Mexico's oldest sanctioned bicycle race?

A. Tour de Los Alamos.

Q. When was Conrad Hilton's La Posada de Albuquerque built?

A. 1939 (it was his first hotel in his home state).

Q. In what city will you find the Executive Secretary/Treasurer of the National Association of Left-Handed Golfers?

A. Española.

Q. Who from Las Cruces was an All-Pro for the Dallas Cowboys before later becoming an avid photographer?

A. Bob Lilly.

Q. What town is home of the southernmost ski area in the United States?

A. Cloudcroft.

Q. What Farmington native has been an ace relief pitcher for the Toronto Blue Jays?

A. Duane Ward.

◆

Q. How many times did Albuquerque resident Bob Foster successfully defend his World Light Heavyweight boxing title?

A. Fourteen.

◆

Q. Who was the founder of Albuquerque's highly regarded Tucker Invitational golf tournament?

A. Dick McGuire, famed golf coach of the University of New Mexico.

◆

Q. When is the Tour de Los Alamos traditionally held?

A. The weekend nearest to the Fourth of July.

◆

Q. What is the nickname of University of New Mexico athletic teams?

A. Lobos.

◆

Q. Who from Tularosa has played baseball for New Mexico State University and the Oakland A's?

A. Steve Ontiveros.

◆

Q. What University of New Mexico All-American center (1964–66) was also an ABA Rookie of the Year and MVP for Minneapolis and star of the Indiana Pacers?

A. Mel Daniels.

Q. The Special Shapes Rodeo, which features a pig, a cow, a polar bear, a penguin, and more, is part of what event?

A. Kodak Albuquerque International Balloon Fiesta.

Q. The Mescalero Apache Indian Reservation is the home of what famous resort?

A. Inn of the Mountain Gods.

Q. Who is the mascot of New Mexico State University?

A. Pistol Pete (aka the Aggie).

Q. How many times has Albuquerque native Bobby Unser won the California 500?

A. Four.

Q. What South American animal is used for some hiking trips in New Mexico's mountains?

A. Llama.

Q. Sandia Peak Tramway carries visitors to what altitude?

A. From 6,500 feet at the base to 10,378 feet at the peak.

Q. Who has won more National Rodeo Finals roping titles than anyone else from New Mexico?

A. Olin Young of Peralta.

Q. According to *Ballparks of North America,* what is the composition of the base paths at Albuquerque Sports Stadium?

A. Sixty percent red mountain clay from Labajada Hill, 25 percent diamond grit (calcified clay), and 15 percent masonry sand.

◆

Q. When was the Alameda Park Zoo established?

A. 1898.

◆

Q. Who from New Mexico has won an Olympic gold medal in the women's 100-meter breaststroke?

A. Cathy Carr.

◆

Q. Los Alamos Mesa Public Library and White Rock Branch, one of the nation's most active library systems, had a circulation of how many items in 1994?

A. More than 409,000.

◆

Q. What University of New Mexico football player of the 1950s held four NCAA kicking return records for twenty years?

A. Chuck Hill.

◆

Q. Who from Albuquerque made the first nonstop crossing of the North American continent in a hot-air balloon?

A. Maxie Anderson.

◆

Q. How many of the state's ten welcome centers are located at exits on New Mexico highways?

A. Five.

Q. What is the second oldest golf course in the state?

A. Los Alamos Golf Course, built in 1948.

———◆———

Q. Where is the highest altitude Olympic-sized swimming pool in the United States?

A. Los Alamos (Larry R. Walkup Aquatic Center, at an altitude of 7,245 feet).

———◆———

Q. What is regarded as "the longest and most grueling" of the bike races in the New Mexico Off-Road Point Series?

A. The Pajarito Punishment.

———◆———

Q. What football player holds the team record at New Mexico State University for most career net yards?

A. Ron "Po" James, with 3,885 yards.

———◆———

Q. What popular Southwestern entrée translates as "little donkey"?

A. Burrito.

———◆———

Q. What is the distance from home plate to the centerfield fence at Albuquerque Sports Stadium?

A. 410 feet.

———◆———

Q. Which two state parks forbid picnicking?

A. Living Desert and Rio Grande Nature Center.

Q. What University of New Mexico basketball star once held eight school scoring records?

A. Toby Roybal.

———◆———

Q. What was notable about Asby Harper of Albuquerque successfully swimming the 28½-mile English Channel on August 28, 1982?

A. At 65, he was the oldest person to do so (his time was 13 hours, 52 minutes).

———◆———

Q. What is the largest rifle range in the world?

A. The Whittington Center in Cimarron.

———◆———

Q. What former New Mexico State gridiron star earned three Super Bowl rings with the Pittsburgh Steelers and is now a coach at his alma mater?

A. Roy Gerela.

———◆———

Q. Who designed Cochiti Golf Course?

A. Robert Trent Jones Jr.

———◆———

Q. What town hosts the New Mexico High School Rodeo Finals?

A. Artesia.

———◆———

Q. What annual event does the Albuquerque-based Married Mothers and Monogamous Males Association sponsor the second weekend of October ?

A. America's Sexy Wives Contest.

Q. How many times has New Mexico's Al Unser Sr. won the Indy 500?

A. Four (1970, 1971, 1978, and 1987).

Q. In which state park can a series of crystal lakes of great depth can be found?

A. Bottomless Lakes State Park.

Q. Who built El Rancho Hotel in Gallup in 1937?

A. R. E. Griffith, brother of film director D. W. Griffith.

Q. What museum is housed in twenty-three buildings in the Palace of the Governors?

A. New Mexico State Museum.

Q. When does the town of Lincoln celebrate Billy the Kid Days?

A. Early August.

Q. What are the three fastest growing sports in the state?

A. Bicycling, rafting, and windsurfing.

Q. Former New Mexico State swimmer Steve Betts received worldwide notice for performing what feat when Iraq invaded Kuwait?

A. Bargaining his way out of Kuwait by giving an Iraqi soldier a six-pack of Diet Pepsi.

Q. As of 1994, how many tennis courts did the county of Los Alamos have?

A. Twenty.

———◆———

Q. Which hotel boasts twenty-nine bullet holes and such former guests as Buffalo Bill Cody, Wyatt Earp, Annie Oakley, and Jesse James?

A. St. James Hotel in Cimarron.

———◆———

Q. The (Kodak) Albuquerque International Balloon Fiesta started in 1972 with 13 balloons. How large is it now?

A. There were 650 balloons from 19 countries in 1995.

———◆———

Q. What golf event named for a former Masters champion is held in Silver City in July?

A. Billy Casper Golf Tournament.

———◆———

Q. What Albuquerquean was an All-NFL flanker back who played for the Eagles, Cowboys, Rams, and Browns during his pro career from 1957 to 1969?

A. Tommy MacDonald.

———◆———

Q. For whom is University of New Mexico's Johnson Gym named?

A. Roy W. Johnson, legendary coach of football, basketball, and track.

———◆———

Q. What former basketball great for New Mexico State University was a teammate of Julius "Dr. J." Erving in both the ABA and the NBA?

A. John Williamson.

Q. Who from New Mexico are the first father and son to compete against each other in the Indy 500?

A. Al Unser Sr. and Al Unser Jr.

———◆———

Q. What golfer raised in Jal holds the LPGA record for the most career victories?

A. Kathy Whitworth, with eighty-eight wins.

———◆———

Q. What is the nickname of athletic teams for Eastern New Mexico State University?

A. Greyhounds.

———◆———

Q. What jockey from Dexter has been honored with an Eclipse Award as the top rider in the country?

A. Mike Smith.

———◆———

Q. Where in the state will you find the Toy Train Depot?

A. Alamogordo.

———◆———

Q. What New Mexico State University football star went on to play in the NFL for the Seahawks and Colts and was nominated for the Pro Football Hall of Fame in 1995?

A. Fredd Young.

———◆———

Q. What are the University of New Mexico's school colors?

A. Cherry and silver.

SCIENCE & NATURE

C H A P T E R   S I X

Q. As of 1994, how many species of amphibians were known to be living in the wild in New Mexico?

A. Twenty-six.

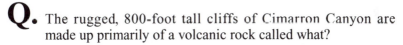

Q. The rugged, 800-foot tall cliffs of Cimarron Canyon are made up primarily of a volcanic rock called what?

A. Mononite.

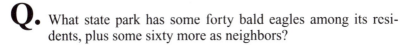

Q. What state park has some forty bald eagles among its residents, plus some sixty more as neighbors?

A. Caballo Lake State Park.

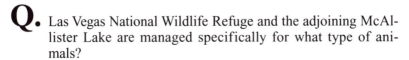

Q. Las Vegas National Wildlife Refuge and the adjoining McAllister Lake are managed specifically for what type of animals?

A. Waterfowl.

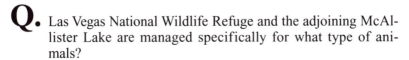

Q. What is Trinity Site?

A. The location, northwest of Alamogordo at White Sands National Monument, where the world's first atomic bomb was tested.

Q. How would a botanist classify New Mexico's popular chile plant?

A. As a fruit.

———◆———

Q. What location in the state has the highest average of annual precipitation?

A. Cloudcroft, with an average of 25.7 inches per year.

———◆———

Q. What is the New Mexico state insect?

A. Tarantula hawk wasp.

———◆———

Q. What New Mexicans were the code talkers of World War II?

A. Navajo Indians who successfully used their native language to confuse Japanese code breakers.

———◆———

Q. What lake attracts more migratory birds each year than any other lake in the state?

A. Ladd S. Gordon Wildlife Preserve, located east of Tucumcari.

———◆———

Q. Who are Moonbeam and Spike?

A. Dinosaur models on permanent display in Clayton.

———◆———

Q. Of the seven life zones on earth, how many can be found in New Mexico?

A. Six (Apline, Subalpine, Mixed Coniferous, Transition, Upper Sonoran Life, and Lower Sonoran Life).

Q. What makes it impossible to see the ghost town of Bonito City?

A. It is under seventy-five feet of water in Bonito Lake (a dam was constructed by Southern Pacific Railroad in Bonito Canyon).

———◆———

Q. What is the world's most sensitive radio telescope system, located near Socorro, called?

A. Very Large Array Telescope.

———◆———

Q. What are the three main types of trees used for commercial timber in New Mexico?

A. Spruce, Douglas fir, and ponderosa pine.

———◆———

Q. What is the Southwest's oldest copper mine?

A. Santa Rita Open Pit Copper Mine.

———◆———

Q. Where in the state is Smokey Bear buried?

A. Capitan.

———◆———

Q. How deep is the Rio Grande Gorge?

A. 650 feet.

———◆———

Q. What is the state's predominant field crop?

A. Cotton.

Q. Of the seventeen species of hummingbirds in the United States, how many can be found in New Mexico?

A. Twelve.

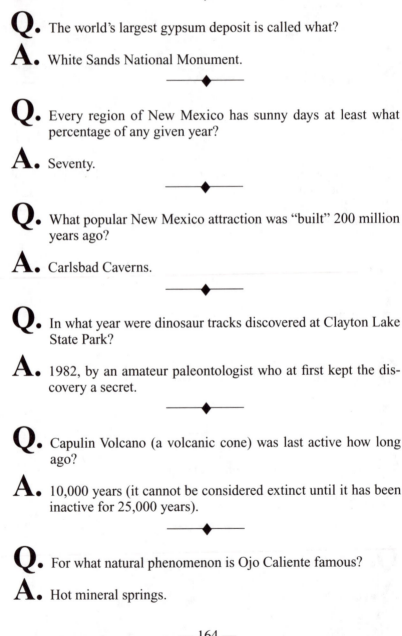

Q. The world's largest gypsum deposit is called what?

A. White Sands National Monument.

Q. Every region of New Mexico has sunny days at least what percentage of any given year?

A. Seventy.

Q. What popular New Mexico attraction was "built" 200 million years ago?

A. Carlsbad Caverns.

Q. In what year were dinosaur tracks discovered at Clayton Lake State Park?

A. 1982, by an amateur paleontologist who at first kept the discovery a secret.

Q. Capulin Volcano (a volcanic cone) was last active how long ago?

A. 10,000 years (it cannot be considered extinct until it has been inactive for 25,000 years).

Q. For what natural phenomenon is Ojo Caliente famous?

A. Hot mineral springs.

Q. What is the wingspan of the average freetail bat, the predominant resident of Carlsbad Caverns?

A. Eleven inches.

———◆———

Q. Is the depth of Carlsbad Caverns greater than the Washington Monument's height?

A. Yes. (The depth of Carlsbad Caverns is more than 1,000 feet, while the Washington Monument is 555 feet high.)

———◆———

Q. As of 1994, how many species of reptiles were known to live in the wild in New Mexico?

A. Ninety-two.

———◆———

Q. When dinosaur tracks were formed at Clayton Lake 100 million years ago, what was the area?

A. The shore of the prehistoric Gulf of Mexico.

———◆———

Q. What was the first wilderness area designated by the U.S. Congress?

A. The Gila Wilderness, in 1924.

———◆———

Q. What national forest surrounds Cloudcroft?

A. Lincoln National Forest.

———◆———

Q. What scientific station is located at Sunspot?

A. One of the world's largest solar observatories.

Q. Between five and eighteen million years ago, twelve species of what animal, ranging in size from that of a modern goat to that of a giraffe, roamed what is now New Mexico?

A. Camel.

———◆———

Q. Eliot Porter of Tesuque is known for his work in what field?

A. Nature photography.

———◆———

Q. Much of New Mexico was covered by water during which prehistoric period?

A. Cretaceous.

———◆———

Q. What is considered to be the best example of a volcanic cone in the state, if not the entire country?

A. Capulin Volcano.

———◆———

Q. What is the deepest known point of Carlsbad Caverns called?

A. Lake of the Clouds.

———◆———

Q. What city was a uranium mining center in 1950 and today is home of the world's only uranium mining museum?

A. Grants.

———◆———

Q. What are the Gilman Tunnels?

A. Tunnels, blasted out of solid rock, used in the 1800s for logging trains.

Q. Outside of Alaska, what forest contains the most federal land?

A. Gila National Forest.

———————◆———————

Q. How did Smokey Bear get his name?

A. As a cub he was singed before his rescue from a 17,000-acre fire in the Capitan Mountains.

———————◆———————

Q. By what nickname is botanist Roy Nakayama of Las Cruces known?

A. Mr. Chile, for his work developing new varieties of the plant.

———————◆———————

Q. Blackwater Draw Site, near Portales, provides evidence of what?

A. That humans, woolly mammoths, and sabertooth tigers all lived during the same time.

———————◆———————

Q. Where is the state's largest petroleum refinery?

A. Navajo Refinery Company in Artesia.

———————◆———————

Q. What plant, prevalent in New Mexico, is also known by the nickname of "Spanish bayonet"?

A. Yucca.

———————◆———————

Q. A hiking rule of thumb is that every one thousand feet of elevation is equivalent to traveling four hundred miles north. In what region would you be if you hiked from the desert base to the top of the Manzano Mountains?

A. Southern Canada.

Q. At what state park are visitors encouraged to take home rocks and gems?

A. Rock Hound State Park.

———◆———

Q. Where is North America's largest salt cedar tree?

A. At almost forty feet tall, it grows along the Rio Grande near Albuquerque.

———◆———

Q. How many species of mammals were known to be living in New Mexico as of 1994?

A. 145.

———◆———

Q. How many bats per minute fly out of Carlsbad Caverns at sundown during the peak of their nightly exit?

A. 5,000.

———◆———

Q. What did Dr. Frank Etscorn, former dean at New Mexico Institute of Mining and Technology, patent?

A. The nicotine patch.

———◆———

Q. What prominent computer software entrepreneurs started their company in Albuquerque in February 1975?

A. Bill Gates and Paul Allen.

———◆———

Q. Where is the largest Alligator Juniper in North America?

A. In the Organ Mountains.

Q. Who in the state was once dubbed the "fastest man on earth"?

A. Dr. John Paul Stapp, who, in 1954 rode the Sonic Wind I rocket sled, whose resulting research data assisted the development of seat belts.

Q. How many species of rattlesnakes might you find in Spring Canyon (Rock Hound State Park)?

A. Four.

Q. Where were the space monkeys, who preceded man in orbit, trained?

A. Holloman Air Force Base.

Q. Vineyards were first planted in New Mexico during what century?

A. Seventeenth.

Q. What do the tracks at Clayton Lake, known as the "dinosaur shuffle," show?

A. A dinosaur hesitating, stepping forward, and stepping backward several times.

Q. What is the largest volcanic caldera in the world?

A. Valle Grande.

Q. Who was the last man to walk on the moon?

A. New Mexico geologist, astronaut, and future U.S. senator Harrison (Jack) Schmitt, in 1972.

Q. Cannon Air Force Base, near Clovis, is the only military unit in the world to operate what two aircraft?

A. F-111E and F-111F.

———◆———

Q. On average, how many cows are milked each day in Curry County?

A. 10,200.

———◆———

Q. Where is the National Atomic Museum located?

A. Kirtland Air Force Base in Albuquerque.

———◆———

Q. Of the fifty species of bats in Carlsbad Caverns, which has the largest population?

A. Mexican freetail, with about one million individuals.

———◆———

Q. Stahmann Farms in the Las Cruces area is one of the world's largest single growers of what crop?

A. Pecans.

———◆———

Q. What is the state flower of New Mexico?

A. Yucca.

———◆———

Q. The Los Alamos Ranch School for Boys was chosen in 1943 to house what?

A. The Atomic Energy Project.

Q. What monolith near Silver City is named for what it looks like?

A. Kneeling Nun.

◆

Q. In 1947, near Roswell, what controversial find was reportedly made?

A. A UFO with spacemen.

◆

Q. Shiprock, a famous New Mexico landmark, is made from what kind of rock?

A. Volcanic.

◆

Q. What is the top speed of a roadrunner, a popular New Mexico bird?

A. Twenty miles per hour.

◆

Q. One the nation's oldest orchards for what fruit overlooks Manzano Lake?

A. Apple.

◆

Q. What city was known as the Pinto Bean Capital of the World until drought hit in the 1950s?

A. Mountainair.

◆

Q. What is Elena Gallegos?

A. A grassland/woodlands habitat on the edge of suburban Albuquerque.

Q. What is the largest lake in New Mexico?

A. Elephant Butte.

———◆———

Q. What is the state bird?

A. Roadrunner.

———◆———

Q. What species of bird flocks in the tens of thousands to Bitter Lake National Wildlife Refuge near Roswell between November and February each year?

A. Snow goose.

———◆———

Q. What is the official mascot of Cienega Canyon?

A. Albert squirrels.

———◆———

Q. The New Mexico-based monkey that flew suborbital in a Mercury capsule was named Ham, which is an acronym for what?

A. Holloman Aero Med (from New Mexico's Holloman Air Force Base).

———◆———

Q. The cat claw shrub is generally about four feet tall, but near Red Rock the largest known specimen is how tall?

A. Fifty feet.

———◆———

Q. What church is believed to have "healing mud"?

A. El Santuario de Nuestro Señor de Esquipulas, in Chimayo.

Q. What is the name for the fossils of the earliest known human inhabitant of New Mexico?

A. Sandia Man.

Q. What are the four colors of Indian corn, all of which are served in New Mexico dishes?

A. Blue, red, white, and yellow.

Q. Roots of the yucca once were commonly used by New Mexico homesteaders for making what?

A. Soap.

Q. What is the Valle Grande?

A. The remains of a volcano that collapsed 1.4 million years ago.

Q. What evidence at Blackwater Draw proved that man lived during the same time as prehistoric animals?

A. A flint spear point imbedded in the leg bone of an Ice-Age mammoth.

Q. When did Albuquerque's National Atomic Museum open?

A. 1969.

Q. Though Sandia Man came to the attention of the anthropology department at the University of New Mexico in 1936, who discovered the evidence?

A. Boy Scouts.

Q. Chaparral cock, medicine bird, lizard bird, churcha cor-recamino, paisano, Clown of the Desert, *geococcyx californi-anus*, and Wile E. meal are all names for what bird associated with the state?

A. Roadrunner.

———◆———

Q. As of 1994, how many species of fish were known to live in New Mexico's waters?

A. 120.

———◆———

Q. What is the state tree?

A. Piñon.

———◆———

Q. Producing one million gallons per day, what does the Saline Water Demonstration Plant east of Roswell do?

A. Investigates ways of changing salt water to pure water.

———◆———

Q. What is La Ventana ("the Window")?

A. A natural arch near Grants.

———◆———

Q. Was the energy of the atomic bombs designed at Los Alamos produced from fusion or from fission?

A. Fission.

———◆———

Q. What is distinctive about New Mexico's herd of oryx (*oryxgazella*)?

A. It is the only herd outside of Africa.

Q. How many dish-shaped antennae make up the Very Large Array near Socorro?

A. Twenty-seven.

Q. What unusual geologic formation will you find in the cinder caves below El Malpais National Monument?

A. Emerald green ice that is twelve to twenty feet thick.

Q. Who is buried near the flagpoles at the International Space Hall of Fame in Alamogordo?

A. Ham, the first chimpanzee in space.

Q. The Siberian Ibex Ram, not native to New Mexico, was first brought to the state from Africa by whom?

A. Dr. Frank Hibben.

Q. How many miles of connecting corridors have been explored in Carlsbad Caverns?

A. Thirty-two.

Q. At an elevation of 10,640 feet in the Magdalena Mountains, the Langmuir Observatory is dedicated to the study of what?

A. The atmosphere.

Q. What scientific facilities are located on the west side of the San Andres Mountains?

A. NASA Apollo Moon Flight Test Facilities.

Q. What modern facilities are on the east side of the San Andres Mountains?

A. White Sands Missile Range.

Q. As of 1994, how many species of birds were known to exist in New Mexico?

A. 485.

Q. What is the diameter of Valle Grande?

A. More than fifteen miles.

Q. What is the world's largest known cave chamber?

A. The Big Room in Carlsbad Caverns, which covers about fourteen acres.

Q. What city is home of the International Space Hall of Fame?

A. Alamogordo.

Q. What company in Rio Rancho employs about as many people as the combined total of the nineteen next largest employers in the city?

A. Computer-chip giant Intel, with more than 4,500 employees.

Q. Where does New Mexico rank among the fifty states for the number of deaths by lightning strikes?

A. Second.

Q. What would a chemist say makes a chile hot?

A. 8-Methyl-N-vanillyl-6-nonenamide (also known as cap-saicin).

Q. From what composition was Soda Dam formed?

A. Deposits of calcium from a carbonite spring.

Q. Where does New Mexico's herd of oryx roam?

A. White Sands Missile Range.

Q. Clayton State Park has preserved footprints of what ancient creatures?

A. Dinosaurs of eight varieties, including the winged ptero-dactyl.

Q. What discovery did Thomas Bopp and Alan Hale of Sixteen Springs make on July 22, 1995, that caught the attention of astronomers around the world?

A. Comet Hale-Bopp.

Q. Where was the operational air base for the first use of motor-ized vehicles and aircraft in warfare by the United States?

A. Columbus.

Q. Who made the first survey of New Mexico's fauna?

A. Castaneda, chronicler for the Coronado expedition in 1540.

Q. When was the first irrigation ditch begun by the Spanish in New Mexico?

A. August 11, 1598, in San Juan.

Q. Who owned the first printing press in New Mexico?

A. Don Ramon Abreu.

Q. The floor of Tularosa Basin is the site of what environmental wonder?

A. White Sands National Monument.

Q. From what variety of plant do tumbleweeds (sometimes used in New Mexico for making snowmen) come?

A. Ripened Russian thistle.

Q. In what year was the first outside telegraph connection made with Albuquerque?

A. 1875.

Q. What are the state "vegetables"?

A. Chile and frijoles.

Q. For whom is Bandelier National Monument named?

A. Adolph Bandelier, Swiss-American ethnologist of the nineteenth century.

Q. What is Trinitite?

A. Sand fused during the atomic-testing detonation at White Sands Missle Range (Trinity Site).

———◆———

Q. What is the highest wind speed ever recorded in New Mexico?

A. 124 mph, at Albuquerque in 1987.

———◆———

Q. What was the main industry of Carlsbad Caverns during the first two decades of the twentieth century?

A. Bat guano mining.

———◆———

Q. What town was the site for liquid-fuel rocket tests by Robert Goddard in the 1930s?

A. Roswell.

———◆———

Q. What building is known as the Golden Cube?

A. The International Space Hall of Fame in Alamogordo.

———◆———

Q. What geologic event happened 1,500 years ago at Valley of Fires?

A. Volcanic eruption and lava flow.

———◆———

Q. Second-place California farms about 2,300 acres of chiles, but how many does New Mexico farm?

A. More than 22,000 acres.

Q. Waterfowl flock by the thousands to what location just south of Socorro?

A. Bosque del Apache National Wildlife Refuge.

———◆———

Q. What volcano is also home of the Ice Cave?

A. Bandera Volcano.

———◆———

Q. Where is the UFO Museum?

A. Roswell.

———◆———

Q. What is the highest recorded temperature in New Mexico?

A. 116°F at Artesia in 1918 and at Orogrande in 1934.

———◆———

Q. What are the nicknames of the two atomic bombs that were built at Los Alamos and helped end World War II?

A. Fat Man and Little Boy.

———◆———

Q. How were the Tent Rocks formed?

A. Erosion of lava.

———◆———

Q. Where does *New Mexico Viewing Guide* say is the best place in the state for viewing yellow-billed cuckoos?

A. Rattlesnake Springs.

Q. What is the New Mexico state fossil?

A. *Coelophysis.*

Q. What city has more Ph.D.'s per capita than any other city in the world?

A. Los Alamos.

Q. What fell out of the sky into the Zuni Reservation on May 10, 1995?

A. An F-117A Nighthawk Stealth fighter plane.

Q. What is the New Mexico state fish?

A. Rio Grande cutthroat trout.

Q. When did Albuquerque's first solar-heated commercial building become functional?

A. 1957.

Q. What university operates New Mexico's Los Alamos National Laboratory for the U.S. government?

A. University of California.

Q. In what year was the dam at Eagle Nest Lake completed?

A. 1916.

Q. What was founded as Project Y of the Manhattan Engineer District?

A. Los Alamos National Laboratory.

———◆———

Q. How much does each dish of the Very Large Array, a scientific instrumentation located near Socorro, weigh?

A. 235 tons.

———◆———

Q. What is the coldest recorded temperature in New Mexico?

A. -50°F at Gavilan in 1951.

———◆———

Q. What is the state gem?

A. Turquoise.

———◆———

Q. On February 15, 1960, at Albuquerque, Jennie Cobb became the first woman to do what?

A. Participate in astronaut testing.

———◆———

Q. What is the deepest cave in the United States?

A. Lechuquilla Cave in Carlsbad Caverns, at 1,565 feet.

———◆———

Q. Where does New Mexico rank among the fifty states in annual per-cow milk production?

A. First, with more than 20,000 pounds per cow.

Q. Where was the hanta virus first recognized?

A. Among Navajo Indians in the Four Corners area in 1993.

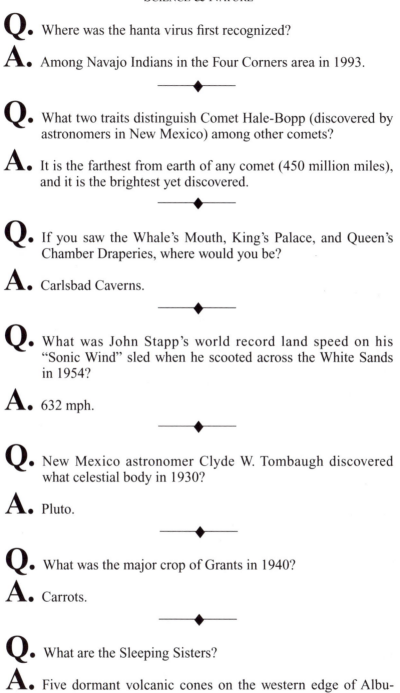

Q. What two traits distinguish Comet Hale-Bopp (discovered by astronomers in New Mexico) among other comets?

A. It is the farthest from earth of any comet (450 million miles), and it is the brightest yet discovered.

Q. If you saw the Whale's Mouth, King's Palace, and Queen's Chamber Draperies, where would you be?

A. Carlsbad Caverns.

Q. What was John Stapp's world record land speed on his "Sonic Wind" sled when he scooted across the White Sands in 1954?

A. 632 mph.

Q. New Mexico astronomer Clyde W. Tombaugh discovered what celestial body in 1930?

A. Pluto.

Q. What was the major crop of Grants in 1940?

A. Carrots.

Q. What are the Sleeping Sisters?

A. Five dormant volcanic cones on the western edge of Albuquerque.

Q. What was the "Roswell Incident"?

A. A UFO crash (alleged) near Roswell in 1947.

◆

Q. What is the name of the building where the first atomic bomb's plutonium core was put together just prior to the test explosion?

A. McDonald House at White Sands Missle Range (it still stands).

◆

Q. What letter best describes the shape of the Very Large Array near Socorro?

A. Y.

◆

Q. What is the largest oil field in the United States?

A. The Permian Basin in southeastern New Mexico and western Texas.

◆

Q. The public is allowed to visit Trinity Site at White Sands National Monument only on the first Saturday of what two months?

A. April and October.

◆

Q. How tall is Soda Dam?

A. Fifty feet.

◆

Q. For what geologic feature is the Bisti Wilderness Area best known?

A. 3,968 acres of oddly eroded shale and sandstone.

Q. What mammal is the state animal?

A. Black bear.

———◆———

Q. What first in rocketry occurred at White Sands Proving Grounds on February 24, 1949?

A. The launch of the first rocket to reach outer space.

———◆———

Q. What has been the most productive uranium mine in the United States?

A. The Rio Algom Company mine in Grants.

———◆———

Q. What Gallup-based group is dedicated to remembering a unique contribution by Navajos to Allied efforts during World War II?

A. Navajo Code Talkers Association.

———◆———

Q. What device has the capacity to produce the highest burst of electric current in the world?

A. The Zeus capacitor at Los Alamos Scientific Laboratory, with double the capacity of anywhere else.

———◆———

Q. What unusual photographs were taken for the first time at White Sands Proving Grounds on March 13, 1959?

A. The first ultraviolet photographs of the sun.

———◆———

Q. What event in New Mexico could be seen 250 miles away, was heard 50 miles away, and reached an altitude of 40,000 feet?

A. The first atomic explosion.

Q. Each August visitors can participate in what special meal at Carlsbad Caverns?

A. Bat Flight Breakfast.

◆

Q. What are New Mexico's Clovis Man, Sandia Man, and Folsom Man?

A. Fossils, each at least 10,000 years old.

◆

Q. What rocket scientist lived in Roswell for eleven years as he developed his liquid propulsion system?

A. Robert Goddard.

◆

Q. Thousands have come to Mrs. Rubio's home in Lake Arthur to see what phenomenon?

A. The shrine containing a tortilla on which the image of Jesus appeared in 1977 while Mrs. Rubio was preparing burritos for Mr. Rubio's lunch.

◆

Q. Where did New Mexico native Smokey Bear live during his years in Washington, DC?

A. National Zoo.

◆

Q. What object of nature is symbolized in the state flag?

A. Zia (sun).

◆

Q. What is the world's longest aerial tramway?

A. Sandia Peak Tramway.

Q. Murray Gell-Mann of Santa Fe coined what scientific term?

A. Quark.

———◆———

Q. What did rancher Paddy Martinez discover in Grants in 1950?

A. Uranium ore.

———◆———

Q. Who is Albuquerque resident Sidney Gutierrez?

A. Former NASA shuttle astronaut and now program manager at Sandia National Laboratories.

———◆———

Q. Apaches and Navajos were forced from their lands throughout the West in the 1860s and marched to New Mexico's Bosque Redondo. What was their legacy to the landscape?

A. 12,000 trees that they planted while in captivity.

———◆———

Q. What major geological feature runs through Gila Canyon?

A. Continental Divide.

———◆———

Q. In 1985, what did Albuquerque residents Arthur Loy, Frank Walker, Jan Cummings, and William Norlander find in the 150 million-year-old Morrison Formation near Albuquerque?

A. The partial skeleton of the longest and largest sauropod (a semiaquatic dinosaur) known at the time.

———◆———

Q. What is the number one crop in the town of Hatch?

A. Chile.

Q. Where in New Mexico can you find more than sixty restored windmills?

A. On the Portales property of Windmill Man Bill Dalley.

Q. Who from New Mexico wrote *The Curve of Binding Energy*?

A. John McPhee.

Q. What was America's second mine to begin an open-pit copper operation?

A. Santa Rita Copper Mines in Silver City.

Q. What is generally regarded by birdwatchers as the best place in the state to observe black-tailed gnatcatchers?

A. Dripping Springs Natural Area.

Q. Whom did J. Z. Knight of Dexter introduce to fellow New Agers?

A. The warrior Ramtha, who is 35,000 years old.

Q. How were the pipes that carry water from the mountains through Whitewater Canyon repaired in 1893?

A. By building the Catwalk, which now serves as a national recreational trail.

Q. Regardless of the temperature outside, what is the temperature inside Carlsbad Caverns?

A. A steady 56°F.

Q. What location has the lowest average annual precipitation?

A. Las Cruces, with an average of eight inches per year.

———◆———

Q. Who established the state's first clinical laboratory equipped with an X-ray?

A. John R. Van Atta, M.D., in 1914.

———◆———

Q. Where in the state will you find the space helmet that Buzz Aldrin wore on the moon?

A. International Space Hall of Fame in Alamogordo.

———◆———

Q. What are Pecos Diamonds?

A. Quartz crystals, favored by rock hounds.

———◆———

Q. Under what condition may a vehicle's horn be outlawed in New Mexico?

A. If it creates an "inharmonious sound."

———◆———

Q. What is the New Mexico's smallest state park?

A. Smokey Bear Historical Park in Capitan (three acres).

———◆———

Q. Approximately how many board feet of lumber are yielded by New Mexico's forests each year?

A. 200 million.

Q. Who built the first atom-smashing cyclotron?

A. Milton Livingston of Santa Fe.

---◆---

Q. Where does New Mexico rank among the fifty states in mineral production?

A. Seventh.

---◆---

Q. What is the largest single mountain in the United States?

A. Sierra Grande (near Folsom), which is an extinct volcano that measures 40 miles around the base, covers 50 square miles, and has an altitude of 8,720 feet.

---◆---

Q. Who is Raunchy Rex?

A. A model *Tyrannosaurus Rex* who travels to events as the town of Clayton's goodwill ambassador.

---◆---

Q. New Mexico is home to officially recognized national champions of what four varieties of trees?

A. Arizona Sycamore (Sierra County), Tamarisk (Columbus), Arizona Walnut (Mimbres Valley), and Torrey Yucca (Lincoln National Forest).

---◆---

Q. The first fusion reaction using electron beams in the United States was achieved in Albuquerque in what year?

A. 1977.

---◆---

Q. What is the nickname of Cabezon Peak in Sandoval County?

A. Big Head.

Q. Approximately how many varieties of wildflowers are known to exist in New Mexico?

A. More than a thousand.

———◆———

Q. What state park is home of Dog Canyon?

A. Oliver Lee Memorial State Park.

———◆———

Q. In what year was Bosque del Apache founded as a National Wildlife Refuge?

A. 1939.

———◆———

Q. During what geological period did most of the present-day New Mexico mountains form?

A. Early Eocene.

———◆———

Q. What New Mexico naturalist wrote *Sand County Almanac*?

A. Aldo Leopold.

———◆———

Q. What is the state grass?

A. Blue Grama.

———◆———

Q. Where is the Meteorite Museum?

A. At the Institute of Meteoritics on the campus of the University of New Mexico in Albuquerque.

Q. How many miles of hiking trails are in Bandelier National Monument?

A. Seventy.

———◆———

Q. What was the resulting body of water from the seventeenth dam built by the U.S. Army Corps of Engineers?

A. Conchas Lake.

———◆———

Q. Little Black Peak Volcano erupted nearly one thousand years ago, forming what state park?

A. Valley of Fires State Park.

———◆———

Q. Before the state adopted "Land of Enchantment," what was its moniker?

A. The Sunshine State.

———◆———

Q. Who captained the first trans-Pacific balloon flight (a journey of 5,200 miles) in November 1981?

A. Ben Abruzzo of Albuquerque.

———◆———

Q. How many miles of public trails are in Carlsbad Caverns?

A. Three.

———◆———

Q. How big is the reservoir (a favorite of sportsmen) formed by Conchas Dam?

A. Twenty-six square miles.